The Art of Persuasion

for Sales Managers

The Art of Persuasion
for Sales Managers

N. C. Christensen

Parker Publishing Company, Inc.

West Nyack, New York

PRINTED IN THE UNITED STATES OF AMERICA
ISBN—0-13-047829-6
B & P

Your Guide to Dynamic Sales Management

This is a "how-to" book written by one who has faced the challenges of executive management responsibilities and who has also tackled the problems of direct selling and mass selling.

This book is aimed directly at the heart of effective sales management. It deals specifically with the power to influence others to produce more sales. It shows how this can be done by mastering the art of persuasion.

Mastery of the art of persuasion can give you dynamic power in the executive field. There is nothing unduly complicated about this. This book is unique in its simplicity.

For instance, your most successful salesman no doubt is quite a persuasive person. Persuasion is such a simple term that we are inclined to pass it over lightly. Nevertheless, persuasion simply means "to influence," or "to win over." Now, that is good selling, isn't it? Is there any reason why this dynamic power should not be released in sales management?

Many salesmen use the art of persuasion in their work every day without giving it a second thought. They have mastered the art. It has become part of their personalities. Their methods of using this power have become second nature to them. This art, which is loaded with power for sales managers as well as for salesmen, merits executive recognition wholly on its power to produce more business.

The principles and techniques herein presented are the products of personal experience, of personal observation and research, of case records, of the achievements of successful sales executives and producing salesmen who have, knowingly or unknowingly, used the art of persuasion.

This book is based on tested, workable methods of putting the art of persuasion to work for you. It shows how to motivate your sales staff to go after business and build sales volume. In addition, this book covers such related subjects as problem-solving, persuasion in leadership, persuasion in communication, persuasion in motivation, persuasion in exploitation, and many others. It deals with persuasion in creating good will and building greater sales volume. It shows how and why persuasion yields dividends.

Sex in selling rates a chapter in this unique book. It explains how and why sales managers can capitalize on man's most formidable rival.

Untried theories about selling and sales management have been ignored. This is a practical, usable book.

The Art of Persuasion for Sales Managers was written with the following objectives: (a) To upgrade the status of the sales manager as an executive, a leader, a teacher, and a producer of sales. (b) To provide the sales manager with "working tools" such as, *ideas for influencing others to sell more;* principles and techniques which are flexible and adaptable *for solving sales management's problems;* principles and techniques which have been tested and have resulted in sales increases. *All this to the glory of persuasive power.*

To this end this book on *The Art of Persuasion for Sales Managers* is dedicated.

N.C.C.

Contents

Chapter 7 continued

chapter 1

How to Generate
Sales Management
Power by Persuasion

Henry J. Kaiser, who had the gift of getting action from his people, was widely known for one little gimmick. This was a sign he kept on his desk. It read: "Don't bring me anything but trouble. Good news weakens me." Kaiser knew what sales managers were up against.

A sales manager is paid to accomplish three things:

1. To establish and maintain sales management influence.
2. To generate selling power in the staff.
3. To produce more sales.

To achieve this three-pronged objective the art of persuasion is an ideal tool for sales managers to use. Through this art salesmen have been inspired to get out of the mediocrity rut. Rather than try to shove salesmen into riches, persuasive sales managers influence them to become top producers. They win them over to the idea of *thinking big.* Doing this the sales manager upgrades his own position. He does so by the power of persuasion which has been the strength of great leaders, even of those in military command. General Walter Krueger once said: "I am always asking my men to do the impossible."

To ask a salesman to perform the seemingly impossible task is a compliment to that salesman. You show that you have confidence in his ability. It is persuasive.

Persuasive sales managers lead their men to victory. They show them how to reach out. They show them the rewards for reaching out for larger stakes. Instead of shouting, "Get out there and start digging!" they figuratively take each salesman by the hand and say: "Come on with me. Let's get our share of that rich ore lying untouched in our territory. How about it?" This appeals to a man's self-interest. He has a motive. As a result he responds to persuasion and he produces.

A favorable image of a sales manager is not the easiest "product" to sell. However, this is the sales manager's burden. He has a selling job on his hands to convince his staff that he is a leader, a motivator, a salesman, a teacher, a problem-solver, and a man in whom they can have faith.

Here are five principles for successful sales management. All have been tested. All are effective:

1. Temper your driving power with heavy doses of persuasiveness.
2. Administer the tonic of persuasion to create a desire within salesmen *to outsell.*
3. Lead more and shove less.
4. Level with your men. Sell yourself to them. Sell the importance to them of their position and of your position.
5. Show more and tell less. Show them how to increase sales. Appeal to their self-interest. A demonstration has far more kick in it than talk. Effective demonstration is the productive tool in all phases of selling.

Everything included in the foregoing five principles pertains to the art of persuasion. It applies to generating sales management power by using persuasion as a fuel. The dynamic power in this gentle art is available to you and to every one of your salesmen. Cultivate this art. Get your salesmen to cultivate it. Together you can reap the rich rewards of persuasive selling and persuasive sales management.

First, the "Mirror Trick" for Persuasive Self-Examination

A speaker at a sales convention suggested that none of us can attain maximum effectiveness unless we have the courage to critically examine ourselves. This doctrine makes sense. He suggested that you and I head for the looking glass as soon as we get up in the morning. He told us to speak up to that impressive figure staring back at us from that mirror. We might say something like this:

"Listen, fellow, what are you up to today? How will you measure up to the problems that will be thrown at you?"

This is the "mirror trick." Those who have tested it agree that it has merit. Why shouldn't we try it? We can ask that guy in the mirror a few pointed questions along this line:

1. How am I, as a sales manager, going to help that man who has been slipping recently? (I realize that his problems are also my problems while he is on my staff.)
2. How am I going to get the boys to jack up our sales? (We're gaining, but we need some extra push.)
3. How can I make more effective use of my time today? (Come to think of it I have been stuffing a lot of unfinished matter into desk drawers lately. I suppose I'll have to break that habit.)
4. How can I muster the courage to write out my good and bad habits in two parallel columns so I can compare them? (Column one for non-productive habits. Column two for productive habits.)
5. What plans do I have to correct my revealed weaknesses? What plans do I have to capitalize on my strong points?

Self-examination is quite different from self-classification. We are first concerned with self-examination. We are concerned with becoming better sales managers. We are concerned with the possibility of having to "remake" ourselves.

In the "mirror trick" we are challenged to apply persuasive power upon ourselves. There are four elements to this challenge: (a) To expose our own weaknesses; (b) to devise ways of correcting those weaknesses; (c) to determine how to become more influential with our salesmen; (d) to determine how to increase our own productivity; (e) to learn more about the art of persuasion in sales management.

If we remain even partial strangers to ourselves we are handicapped to a certain extent. By consistent use of the "mirror trick" or some suitable alternate for self-examination we can become more effective sales managers. We can learn the art of becoming more persuasive and more inspiring to salesmen. Our objective: To persuade our sales staffs to get out and chalk up sales records which will benefit them and yield dividends for us.

A veteran sales manager who thought he knew all of the tricks tried the "mirror trick." This is what happened, as he told it to a group of his colleagues:

"I found that honest self-examination was the most profitable step I had ever taken. I *discovered* that little annoying things which some of my salesmen did were the same faults that I had. I *discovered* that by honest self-examination I gradually became less arrogant. I wasn't so cocksure any more. *I became more exacting with myself. The pay-off:* I found out how to get more out of my sales staff, how to accomplish more myself and how persuasion figured in all of this improvement."

Principle: (An old one) "Physician, heal thyself."

Six Revealing Slots for Self-Classification

Self-interest is the primary incentive for self-classification. Self-interest motivates a sales manager to persuade his staff to top last month's sales record. Self-classification and self-examination are copartners in total development for effective executive management.

Suppose you have written off that ancient named Disraeli, making a snap judgment that he could not have had any idea of today's problems. On that basis you may have sold Disraeli short. It was he who uttered this bit of wisdom which might contain a kernel of value for sales managers:

"A man can know nothing of mankind without knowing something of himself. Self-knowledge is the property of that man whose passions have full play, but who ponders over their results."

Isn't it possible for you, as a sales manager, to give your passion for greater sales volume full play? Isn't it also probable that by knowing more about the capacity of your sales staff that you may come to know more about yourself?

We are dealing here with a more critical form of self-examination—self-classification. Executives seem to fall into six significant classifications—into three pairs of opposites. Here they are. Check them and relate them to the man who is the most important one to us at this moment—*you:*

1. Self-confident	1a. Unsure
2. Imaginative	2a. Realistic
3. Impulsive	3a. Patient

This form of self-examination lays bare your strengths as well as your weaknesses. It enables you to attain mastery over yourself, to become more persuasive, thereby exerting greater influence upon others.

One sales manager rode the crest of success in a spectacular automobile enterprise on the Pacific coast. Then a bad month snapped at him. Then another popped into the picture. This self-confident man immediately saw that confidence was not enough. His self-confidence had been nourished by a rising market. But this was a reversal. He faced a crisis. He became unsure of himself. He felt the pain of this uncertainty. But he took himself in hand. In effect, he did the "mirror trick." He faced up to his weakness. This alone gave him strength. He began to see the difference between self-confidence and over-confidence. By frank self-examination and self-classification he pulled out of this crisis victorious and with a double profit:

1. He got sales volume up again.
2. He discovered the weak spots in himself and in his sales staff and kept his sales volume on the uptrend.

The sales manager of a department store chain was on the carpet for lack of enterprise. He was a cold, calculating, realistic man—devoid of imagination. He produced figures for a critical board of directors. These figures showed consistent, steady volume.

"What plans do you have for the future?" asked the chairman of the board. "What problems do you foresee?"

"Surely these figures speak for themselves," replied the sales manager.

The general manager suggested: "We have a new competitive situation now. They are expanding into our territory. They are bound to tap what has been a rich source of business for us. Isn't that reasonable?"

The question struck a sensitive nerve in the sales manager. Until then he had basked in the comfort of past performance. He hadn't been looking ahead. This he now realized. He had been observing the competitive activity but until this moment he really hadn't seen the challenge in it. He, too, did some sort of "mirror trick" and got hold of himself. He came up with a persuasive, imaginative sales program which delighted the board. By self-examination, self-classification and self-persuasion he did more than meet a competitive threat. He outdistanced it.

The sales manager for a syndicate which produced promotional aids had hundreds of salesmen covering a variety of potential markets in every state in the nation. They were getting volume but sales costs were out of bounds. This soaring overhead could not continue, the sales manager reasoned. He found the weak spot. Heavy turnover in the sales force had increased training costs. Trainees also sold less than salesmen in the harness. At this point this sales manager also did the "mirror trick." This revealed that his own impulsiveness was responsible for much of the excessive turnover in the staff. Further self-examination convinced this sales manager that greater self-control was in order. He made the necessary turn-about and solved his problem.

We have introduced the "mirror trick" as a tool for self-examination. We have also introduced six classifications of executives. We may profit further by examining various types of sales managers who have been in the

This Is Your Self-Classification Check List

Various Types of Sales Managers	Applies to me	Does not apply to me
Bulldog Type—Barks but seldom bites.		
Perfectionist—Tolerates no gray areas. It's either black or white. Reluctant to delegate duties.		
Professional—Pride in his calling; inspiring; persuasive.		
Idea-Producer—Imaginative; creative.		
Skeptical "Show Me" Type—Man of wavering faith.		
Arrogant—"Do it my way or else."		
Back-Slapper—Bubbles over with friendliness.		
Astute—Calm; dignified; exacting.		
Austere—A slowly moving iceberg.		
Martinette—Pompous. Fires instructions in machine-gun fashion. A "spit and polish" chap.		
Firm—Yields only when a better way is offered.		
Warm—Depth of interest in others.		
Confident—Deals in truths, facts. Rarely guesses.		
Easy-Going—Evades deep thinking. Dodges worry.		

commercial spotlight for some time. As you check this list ask these questions about each of the types of sales managers listed:

—Does this image apply to me?

—Why does it?

—Why doesn't it?

—If I am this type do I impress my sales staff favorably or unfavorably?

—If I am this type do I impress my sales staff at all?

After you have chosen your type (and have made your self-appraisal) then ask these questions:

—In what way does this give me leadership strength?

—In what way should this inspire my sales staff to strive for greatness?

—In what way can I improve upon this situation?

—How can I become more persuasive and more productive?

—Does falling into this category indicate weakness or strength in me?

—What more can I personally do to make myself a more persuasive person and a more productive sales manager?

Capitalizing on Your Weaknesses by Persuasion

Weakness can become an asset through persuasion. The art of persuasion has dual power. You can turn it inward (on yourself) or outward (on the other fellow). Either way, mastery of the art of persuasion pays off in sales management.

This is the formula for *capitalizing* on your weakness:

1. Root out your chief weakness. Expose it to yourself. Use the "mirror trick" for critical self-examination.
2. When you become acquainted with your chief weakness don't attempt to conceal it. Accept this burden. Determine to overcome it.
3. If you wish, confide in someone. Choose someone capable of understanding your problem and advising you.
4. Set up a persuasive step-by-step plan to knock out this demon. Work that plan to the limit.
5. Learn to bring pressure to bear upon your weakness. Have the courage to do so. Devise ways of your own to change weakness into positive strength.

Out of hundreds of case records we have chosen five examples of how other sales managers have capitalized on their weaknesses through persuasive effort. Here are those examples:

No. 1—Weak in Person-to-Person Communication

This sales manager headed up a sales force in the moving and storage business. He began as a salesman. He made only a passing grade. Knocking on doors, trying to beat competition through executive doors was not his dish. Timidity slowed him down. Top management, however, recognized this man's built-in capacity. They were willing to bet on him. They threw him into an executive spot and buried him under an avalanche of responsibilities. They made him acting sales manager to fill a vacancy caused by transfer. This man stepped into that spot with this advantage: He had already taken the first step toward conquering his weakness. He had admitted it.

Then one day he called a salesman into his office. There he discovered something that gave him strength and his timidity fled. He was on his own ground talking face-to-face with, not a prospect, but a man working for him. He had no strange doors to open, no resistance from more aggressive competitors. All this gave him confidence. He enjoyed this sort of person-to-person communication. He began building a new structure atop his weakness. He became a very persuasive executive. This once timid soul stepped up from acting sales manager to sales manager and then on to general sales director. He had found his own way to become strong in an area where he had been weak.

No. 2—Weak on Group Communication

This sales manager was in insurance and had built a high volume record in personal selling. The executive spot was different, however. Sales conferences, executive meetings, all forms of public speaking horrified him. He knew his weakness. He even made light of it to his associates. One day he opened up to his physician. The doctor listened. When this sales manager had talked himself out his doctor asked: "What are you afraid of? You're not a coward, are you? The people in your audience are not terrorists, are they? If you should blunder, don't you suppose they would forgive you? Here's what I'd do: I'd get all excited about my subject and go into my next meeting with my chin out. I'd speak out with authority. I'd pound the podium with my fist to emphasize a point. I'd practice on the men who work for me. I'd talk to them as though I really meant it. You know, action will restore your confidence in yourself. I don't know who kicked it out of you, but you can get it back by your own effort."

This sales manager did exactly what the doctor ordered and he restored his confidence in himself. He became a whiz as a sales manager. He also became a much sought-after public speaker. He had persuaded himself to do something about his weakness.

No. 3—Weak on Written Communication

This sales manager's memorandums to the staff and to other

executives in an expanding automobile agency were models of bad communication. He could get on his feet and talk. But, write? No. He recognized his weakness. Because of it he cut down on memos and letters. He discovered that this was injuring him because he was losing out in communication with those he should keep in touch with. The obvious solution to his problem seemed too simple. There was a veteran secretary in the house who had reached the age when secretaries get pushed around to make way for the glamour girls. He went to this woman and persuaded her to pull him out of his difficulty. She was flattered. He had little difficulty in getting her transferred to his department. She became his "written mouthpiece." She put his instructions and his criticisms into persuasive and tactful language. In time, this sales manager also learned from this veteran secretary how to write as clearly as he spoke. In this way he built upon his weakness and capitalized on it.

No. 4—Weak in Follow-Through

This sales manager's pasture was a four-state territory. He was in the building supply business and directed a crew of traveling salesmen. One week several sales of substantial size slipped away from him. His chief competitor got the business. This sales manager's salesmen had been out-bid by competition because of their sales manager's weakness—failing to follow through. He had failed to get revised prices to them. He, too, resorted to the "mirror trick." Self-examination revealed to him that he had made a clerk out of himself instead of an executive. Too much detail meant that he had been hoarding vital material, such as price changes, which should get out to the men in the field without delay. The solution to his problem was simpler than he had at first imagined. He delegated this detail work to his secretary. She was happy, too. She had wanted to get into those over-stuffed drawers in her boss's desk, but hadn't dared. With this simple delegation of responsibility this man capitalized on his weakness. Underneath this change in attitude toward the job to be done was the power of persuasion at work. It affected the sales manager, his secretary, and his staff in the field.

No. 5—Weak on Patience

This sales manager created an image which may be familiar to you. He represented a firm which created and produced fine home furnishings. It was his responsibility to maintain an effective sales force to move the factory's products. This impatient man spread the germ of uneasiness to all he contacted. In time, the reality of this weakness brought stubborn problems to him. His salesmen avoided him. They came only when he sent for them. He wondered why. The "mirror trick" failed to expose to this man his weakness. The reason: He was too impatient, too irritable to do an honest, in-depth job of self-examination. He "lost his cool" one day when a low production report from one of his field men came to his desk. He phoned for the man to be there in the morning.

"Are you always late for appointments?" the upset sales manager barked at the man when he came in.

"Seldom, except here," the salesman replied, and smiled.

"Except here?" the sales manager repeated. "Tell me—what gives among the men? You, for instance. You're never late, except when I call you. The others never come in unless I call for them. We can't get anywhere with that sort of team. What's wrong?"

"You," the salesman shot back. "I'm ready to leave the firm. So are three others. You're too impatient, Mr._____. You're too unreasonable. We never have the opportunity to discuss the problems in the field with you."

That night this sales manager got serious about the "mirror trick." Never before had he seriously examined himself. What he learned by this critical self-examination made him impatient with himself. He persuaded himself to change. He got around to taking his salesmen into his confidence. He admitted to them that he had been unreasonable. He persuaded them to go after business with the assurance that they would be backed up by him and by the firm.

By persuasive action he changed his seething impatience into creative, idea-packed energy. This paid dividends three ways: (a) it paid off for him; (b) it paid off for the firm he represented; (c) it paid off for his selling team.

This impatient sales manager's success in capitalizing on his weakness supports what Rousseau, the French philosopher, once said:

"Patience is bitter, but the fruit is sweet."

Persuasive Ways to Cash in on Your Strength

You have already pinpointed your strength. You did this by the "mirror trick" when you put your finger on certain strong points which you recognized. You then examined yourself and classified yourself.

You are now ready to cash in on your self-examination and on your self-classification. You should capitalize on your strength. For example, let us examine five strong points taken from the chart previously presented. Are these among your strong points? Let us explore the following and see how we can capitalize on them:

1. Convincing and believable qualifications.
2. Leadership qualifications.
3. Creativity—a source of ideas.
4. Problem-solving ability.
5. Time-conservationist—efficiency.

Convincing

The convincing and believable sales manager is a sharp contrast to the four-flusher. There is a calm persuasiveness in the believable executive; he creates confidence. Opportunities for cashing in on this strong point come up frequently. The calm, persuasive sales manager gets higher production out of his staff. He has a subtle drive which gets action. He generates within others a desire to achieve—his sales staff catches his spirit. The strong, convincing, believable sales manager shares with his staff in the resultant harvest which is a product of persuasive sales management.

A cement block production enterprise with excellent growth potential struck a low point in sales. A new sales manager took over. His first step was to get approval to close down everything for a two-hour general session of all employees. In this single act he established communication beyond the sales staff. He took the whole force into the selling team. He served coffee and doughnuts and then got his message across. He had a convincing plan. He was a persuasive man. He spoke with the men and women on a personal basis. The reaction afterward was that the production force, the office force, the sales force and the others believed him when he said all of them had a part in selling what was made in the plant. They responded: Sales climbed, production increased, and the firm became significant in the market. Its revitalized strength, a product of persuasive sales management, became the chief topic of conversation in market circles.

Creativity

If you cast your lot with the creative group in sales management you let yourself into the most challenging of all fields. You become the "idea factory" of the firm. From you flows new, salable ideas for securing more business, for expanding markets, for improving products. You come up with more advanced ideas for training your sales force. You agree that this is strength? That's your first step toward further testing of the power of persuasion in sales management. Should you succeed in this broad field you have pictured they will call you the "spark plug" of the business. You should succeed if you are creative. That's the companion power of the art of persuasion. You can go the limit with this combination.

Leadership

No doubt you realize that there are several types of leaders. We have the bull dog type, the arrogant leaders, and also the perfectionists. Do any of these fit in your case? Such leaders hold down their jobs and they get business. Then we have the warm, creative leaders. We also have the firm, professional sales managers. They also get the job done in their respective ways. You see, your personality determines how you will exercise leadership. Making the most of your strong points is a personal problem. But thoroughly knowing your strength is an advantage. You get this knowledge by critical self-examination. In one way or another the art of persuasion and its power will get into your progress picture.

Problem-Solving

As a problem-solver you have set yourself up as a confidante for those who work for you, for those for whom you work, and for those to whom you sell. They come to you with their problems. The more they believe in you, the more they rely on you. This indicates your persuasive power. They may come fearing they are sinking. You will steer them into shallow waters; you will show them a beachhead. You inspire them; you make successes out of near-failures. You cash in by sharing their victories over themselves. You inspire them to sell more. By assisting customers to solve their problems you encourage them to buy more and sell more of your products. By assisting your firm in solving its problem you secure your future.

But you, too, will have personal problems. As a self-classified problem-solver you probably face such problems calmly. You resist panic. You persuade common sense to take over. You dissect your problem and examine it, dispassionately, in all its ugliness. Then, and not until then, do you proceed to solve it.

One industrialist put the problem-solving problem in this light: "Some say there are insurmountable problems, but I don't believe it. You may think your problem is unsolvable, but insurmountable? Never. If a problem cannot be profitably solved at once, set it aside. Get on with more productive jobs calling for immediate attention. Frequently those 'unsolvable' problems have a habit of coming out of their hiding places. They come back dressed in new attire. You may even welcome the reappearance of these old problems because the solution is so embarrassingly obvious."

The combination of time and calm, thoughtful approach to a problem gives it reality. And the reality of a problem often becomes the most persuasive power in solving it.

Efficiency

This may be another strong point which you credited to yourself. Efficiency has many meanings to many people. However, the really efficient executive usually is a dedicated time-conservationist. As Arthur Brisbane wrote: "Every minute that you save by making it useful, more profitable, is so much added to your life and its possibilities." That is one way you can cash in on your strength as a time-conservationist. Thomas A. Edison was a time-conservationist. He was also creative, persuasive, and a realist. This combination added millions of dollars worth of new ideas to the world. These ideas had persuasive qualities and those persuasive qualities made them salable.

The Secret of Cashing In

Your challenging task as a sales manager is to equip your salesmen with the "tools of their trade"—desirable, useful, helpful, beneficial *ideas* about using your products. Your salesmen will also need to receive from you a fuel known as enthusiasm. Convert this fuel into persuasive power and you get dynamic salesmanship—the persuasive way for you to cash in on your strength as a sales manager.

Five Points for Strengthening Executive Control

The executive sales director of a diversified publishing concern was a genius in the art of drawing sub-executives close to him. Few written directives emanated from his office. His genius in maintaining and strengthening executive control was vested in face-to-face communication. He used the phone as a quick communication tool. His instructions were brief, understandable. His phone call usually ended with this crisp final requirement: "See me in the morning. I'll have more details for you then."

His system had persuasive power—it got action under way at once. He set an early, specific time for a follow-through. By telling and retelling (phone and face-to-face) he implied urgency to what he had in mind. To these preliminary steps he added definite schedules for progress reports.

He kept all communication lines up between himself and his subordinates. He strengthened executive control by constant, pleasant, persuasive pressure for results.

The following five points are vital for executive control:

1. By attitude and conduct, upgrade the image of the sales manager's position and the overall importance of his office.
2. Promote loyalty by demonstrating loyalty. Encourage loyalty in the staff to the sales manager and to the house he represents by reflecting deep understanding of the individual salesman's problems and a sincere interest in his welfare.
3. Preview policy changes prior to enunciating those policies. "Sell" the staff on the "why" of the changes and what the new policy will mean to them. Wherever possible stress the benefits. This is persuasion.
4. Deal promptly and firmly with infractions of the rules or policies of the house. Be equally prompt to praise or otherwise reward those who perform meritorious service.
5. Be persuasive. Through this art others are influenced to *want to do* what we desire them to do.

The sales manager of a specialized operation in commercial and residential remodeling gained wide recognition for executive control and consistent sales progress. His staff consisted of ten salesmen and three salesmen-estimators. He was a pleasant fellow. He radiated friendliness and still he kept the reins tight enough for executive control. "Persuasive dignity" was one outstanding quality of this man. This may have contributed to his high production record. His whole operation demonstrated the power of persuasion in sales management.

The "Miracle Power" in Persuasion for Boosting Sales

The heavy line on your sales graph climbing steadily upward is a beautiful thing in the eyes of a sales manager. Behind that upward trend is a "miracle power." Time and again this "miracle" has proved its effectiveness in creating and maintaining sales volume. This "miracle power" is the *art of persuasion.*

Those who may have pooh-poohed the idea of the power of persuasion probably have not observed this art in operation. "Miraculous" results have, in fact, been achieved by persuasive selling and by persuasive sales management. There is no mystery about this. The art of persuasion is simply inducing others to *want* to do what we would *like* to have them do. Case records show that this art is ideally suited to more effective sales management.

These three simple steps have been found to be effective for persuading salesmen to sell more, which is the dream of sales managers:

1. *Take the salesman into your confidence.* Convince him that you are interested in him and in his progress. Get him to unburden himself. If he can unload part of his personal problems (or his gripes) he may be in a better mood to listen. Sell him on the "miracle power" of persuasion in selling. Do this by persuasive selling on your part.

2. *Instead of chastising the salesman* for falling down on his last bid for a piece of desirable business, try to find out how or why he lost out. He may not really understand why or how he failed. But get him to talk. Once he opens up there is no telling what tips, or even what wisdom, may pour out from his lips. This, too, is the art of persuasion for sales managers in action.

3. *Show your salesman how he can double his income* in the next 90 days. You're now reaching out for his self-interest. That's persuasive. Show him case records of how others have been "writing their own tickets." You're getting close to him. Of course he wants to earn more. You have an investment in him. You want him to succeed. Is he worth trying to develop? Or, should you drop him and take on a new problem? You decide to stick with this fellow. In this your own self-interest governs your thinking. You see, persuasion has been at work on you while you were trying to persuade the salesman to do better. What happened to persuade you to give this man another chance? He simply responded favorably to your own persuasive power. He opened up and told his own story so convincingly that you lost your doubts of him. At this point it was your moment for effective persuasive action on him. This is what other sales managers have done with this "miracle power":

(a) They have shown salesmen how to make their sales approaches more persuasive.

(b) They have demonstrated rather than talked about how to make sales presentations more persuasive.

(c) They have shown how the best closers are closing even more sales by turning on the "miracle power"—the art of persuasion.

(d) They have used persuasive methods in testing problem salesmen to determine if problem salesmen are fully sold on the value of persuasion in selling.

These three steps for persuading salesmen to sell more are aimed directly at the self-interest of both salesman and sales manager. The "miracle power" called the art of persuasion is made up of such elements—search for those elements and use them persuasively.

chapter 2

How to Increase
Sales Leadership
Power by Persuasion

Sales management and the art of persuasion are so closely linked that you might call them twins.

An industrial executive who had climbed to the top rung in the management ladder by dynamic leadership power said:

"Sales management is the most vital spot in our organization. Without all the qualities which effective sales management calls for this industry cannot long survive as a leader in its field." To this he added that among record-breaking sales managers he had known all of them had these three qualities:

1. Effective Discipline.
2. Personal Interest in the Welfare of Each Member of His Staff.
3. Persuasive Power.

Examine those areas. Within those three areas lie opportunities for increasing your sales leadership power.

Discipline may be a harsh word. It does have stern implications. It can also be most persuasive. Some disciplinarians are calm, considerate, soft-spoken executives. They maintain tight reins by using *persuasive discipline.* Instead of thumping their desks and screaming: "We don't do it that way!" they say, "Let me show you how we handle this problem. You'll find this way is more productive and more profitable to you." That's the soothing method of discipline.

The salesmen you are charged with "managing" are your major assets. You are supposed to teach them, to direct them, to control them. Yours is an objective assignment. Unless they produce you fall down. If they do produce you soar to new heights. And, *they will produce.* They will respond to sales leadership which is administered by a sales manager knowledgeable in the art of persuasion.

The sales manager of a brewery had built and maintained its regional sales volume through two types of salesmen: (a) truck driver salesmen; and (b) field salesmen. The truck driver salesmen were the immediate concern of this sales manager. They were the men who could see expansion possibilities along their routes in wide-open rural spaces. They were the men on whom the sales manager depended to sell his beer to likely and desirable dealers along the way. He taught those driver-salesmen the art of persuasion in selling and how it would pay off for them. He provided them with specialty items to be used as entering wedges in their calls. Such specialties included key cases with bottle openers, ash trays with the brewery's imprint, pocket books, and ball-point pens. The driver's name was imprinted on the specialties he had to pass out. In this way they had persuasive power. They were personal items. The driver-salesmen were proud to present these items to prospective buyers. This was a minor contribution to the support of his salesmen but in doing this personal thing the sales manager demonstrated how the art of persuasion can increase sales leadership power.

Sales management is an impressive title. It is also a challenging title. Sales management has deeper significance than a new name plate on your door or on your desk. It implies: "This is where dynamic leadership takes over."

Sales management becomes vital the moment leadership qualities in the sales manager take over. In "taking over," sales managers might profit by assuming the same attitude that Lord Nelson had in his position. Lord Nelson was not a sales manager per se. He was a British admiral and he did demonstrate considerable persuasive power. This was his attitude: "I am not come for to find difficulties, but to remove them."

When you took over as sales manager you hopefully did not set out to uncover difficulties as your top priority project. Hopefully, also, you set about removing the difficulties that stared at you. They were your emergency problems. They were holding up progress. In effect, these emergency problems were crying out to you:

"We need leadership power to subdue us."

Increasing sales leadership power by persuasion amounts to "selling the idea" to those who do the selling. J. Paul Austin, as president of the Coca-Cola Co., put it this way:

"This is an unusual company," Mr. Austin was quoted as saying. "The people in it are really dedicated to what they're doing and take a unique attitude toward the company—a very serious attitude—and regard their jobs as more than just a paycheck."

The art of persuasion can be your means of increasing your sales leadership power in sales management.

How to Create Business by Persuasive Leadership

"Make it happen" is more than a slogan. It is the philosophy of dynamic sales managers who are creating business by persuasive leadership. The "make it happen" spirit refuses to be satisfied with twiddling thumbs because "everything seems to be going all right." Make it happen" is a battle-cry for action—creative, constructive, persuasive action.

Persuasive leadership for creating business can be accomplished through closer contact with the source of sales. It requires closer contact with salesmen in the field. It virtually demands closer contact with those to whom you anticipate selling your wares. Are your salesmen doing a persuasive selling job, day in and day out? Or don't you really know? To feel the pulse of your sales staff and the pulse of potential buyers you have to get near to them.

For a long time a floor covering concern maintained a steady, level line across its sales chart. This steady, level line worried a management consultant who was retained by top management to look into the business health of the firm. The consultant said that he probably would not be as concerned if the sales chart had shown some hills and valleys. But, a constant, level performance indicated to him no progress, no challenge.

After further study the management consultant called in a salesman with more than ten years of service with the company. He asked him:

"If you were sales manager of this concern what would be the first thing you would do?"

The salesman felt he had been put on the spot. He hesitated. However, he finally replied: "I'd get out of this office a lot. I'd get out and see how my salesmen worked. I'd find out what they were up against. I'd make calls with my salesmen and get to know the people to whom they sold and to whom they hoped to sell. I'd find out all I could about those customers and potential customers."

Not bad for a salesman who was reluctant to answer a direct question. He may not have realized it at the moment but he had shown what the management consultant evaluated as sound thinking.

Digging further into the operation of this concern the management consultant discovered that:

- —The present sales manager had been in the field only once since he took over the job.
- —The present sales manager's insight into marketing problems in the territory served by the firm was superficial.
- —Many of the salesmen, some with excellent potential, were merely taking orders instead of doing a persuasive selling job.

Several months later the ten-year veteran in selling took over the sales manager's chair in this firm. The first thing he did was to get away from the office and get out into the field, just as he had suggested. Some tangible results came from this rather simple step:

(a) His presence in the territory perked up the salesmen. They were getting attention from the home office. Their jobs took on new importance to them. Their attitude changed.

(b) The executive call was appreciated by customers and potential customers. Their importance in the market had also been recognized. This pleased them.

(c) The new sales manager personally profited. He returned to his office with a feeling of closeness to his field salesmen. He had a deeper understanding of their problems. He gained an insight into marketing problems of customers and potential customers.

The general agent of an insurance firm came into his position with a top rating in personal sales. As a general agent he was, in effect, a sales manager. As a salesman he had been persuasive. In his new position he turned this persuasive power on his sales staff. He inspired them go after the tough accounts, to roll up the worthwhile business. This sales-producing general agent advocated a 5-point scope of interest for sales managers generally:

1. Become personally interested in each salesman on your staff. Know about his family, his problems, his aspirations.

2. Become intensely interested in what you have to sell. Become an authority on its uses, its value to buyers. Encourage salesmen to seek out new fields for marketing the product. Encourage salesmen to suggest how your product might be improved, new ways in which it might be used with

benefit to the buyer, new ways in which it could be marketed more profitably.

3. Become constructively interested and active in affairs of your community, your state, your church, your country. *Encourage your salesmen to do likewise.*

4. Become more interested in the welfare of your neighbors and those whom you serve. *Encourage your salesmen to do likewise.*

5. Set up a goal based on some formula such as this: Make today more productive than yesterday. Make tomorrow more productive than today. *Encourage your salesmen to do likewise.*

The foregoing formula is uncomplicated. It is, in fact, rather simple. This doesn't depreciate its value. This successful sales executive was bluntly telling us to get out of our ivory towers and mix with people.

To all of this the art of persuasion is directly related. Perhaps the principle of persuasive leadership can stand some amplification. Let us not be misled. Persuasion and persuasiveness do not imply coddling. This art is not a soothing syrup to be administered to those too indifferent to strike out and use their own power. We who are in executive spots can profit individually by pondering what Abraham Lincoln said about leadership:

"You cannot help men permanently by doing for them what they could and should do for themselves."

When a salesman shows desire to lift himself up above mediocrity he hurls a challenge at his sales manager. At that moment the sales manager will show the power of his persuasive sales leadership. He will couple his persuasive leadership to his creative strength to generate power for creating more business.

Five Persuasive "Pitches" Which Stimulate Salesmen

An aggressive sales manager called his field men in one day to announce the new products coming on the market. After a brief introduction he asked his sales force if this wasn't true:

"Today's salesmen are better informed than salesmen of the past."

He got his answer—a chorus of "Yeas."

This sales manager didn't buy all of their self-confidence as a package. "I'll agree," he told them, "that you may be better informed than salesmen of the past. But, there is more to be informed about. I want to make this point: We still don't know enough. So we ought to avoid getting all puffed up about our knowledge. There is so much more to know. Let's go after it. We'll need it in this competitive market. You can't get overfed on knowledge." This sales manager was aiming straight at his target. He was needling his men to keep them on their toes. In time, however, he learned that he too had to guard against having the spigot of knowledge turned off for him. He found out that he needed to have a constant flow of knowledge to meet the demands of his position. He needed to be kept informed of the capabilities of his men. He needed to know the sort of tonic that would give them increased selling power. He became acutely aware that he needed market knowledge, too, to maintain his sales leadership power.

To stimulate salesmen here are five "pitches" which have produced productive results:

1. An appeal to personal pride.
2. An appeal to pride in what they have to sell.
3. An uplifting "shot" to reinforce their self-confidence.
4. Recognition of accomplishment and of loyalty.
5. An invitation to voice criticism and complaints.

One sales manager who directs more than 50 field salesmen has high regard for the persuasive power in pride. In one instance he turned a slipping salesman into a productive salesman. The salesman alerted the sales manager when he skipped one daily report. When he skipped another one the sales manager took action. He went out to see that salesman. He didn't shatter the salesman's pride. He made calls with the salesman. He met buyers with whom the salesman dealt. This added prestige to the salesman's position. The day he visited the salesman turned out to be a good day, saleswise. That night the sales manager asked the salesman about the two "lost days." The salesman was frank in his explanation. "I was ashamed to send in a blank report. So I sent none. I think that contributed to a second blank day because I worried about the first blank day and making no report. I guess I was too chicken to take it. But I'm real proud of the business I wrote today."

Principle: Pride has persuasive power. Appeal to it. Sometimes appeal to it by remaining silent as the sales manager in the foregoing case did.

If a man lacks pride in himself he won't sell. If he lacks pride in what he has to sell he might "peddle" it, but he won't really hit the ball and sell it. Stimulating pride in what his salesmen have to sell presents to a sales manager an opportunity to demonstrate how persuasive he can be. Until the sales manager gets excited about a product his salesmen are apt to view it with unproductive calmness. When the sales manager gets excited himself about a product and about his salesmen who sell it, then things begin to happen. His salesmen find buyers. His product moves in quantity and his record as a producing sales manager makes him puff up a bit with pride.

If your salesmen are proud of what they are doing, of what they are selling, and if they are proud of themselves as men of accomplishment, then *self-confidence* follows as naturally as day follows night. Self-confidence is the dawn for those salesmen who have needed stimulating. The light of self-confidence tells them that they do amount to something. They become convinced that they can achieve more than they are doing. When sales managers play on this sensitive chord they produce highly productive salesmen. This is what sales management power is all about. It is a product of artful persuasion.

To praise a man for loyalty calls for a measure of diplomatic judgment. The compliment falls flat if you slap him on the back and say: "It's great to have a loyal man like you on my team." You can get through to your men more impressively by doing as one sales manager I knew did. Whenever a salesman closed a much-wanted sale against great competitive odds that sales manager would turn the spotlight on that man. "Take a look at this man's record," he would tell his staff. "This is how Jim got this piece of business. I'm betting he'll score other victories, too. He just believed he could land that business, and he did. He also believed just as strongly about what he was selling. Don't you see, men, that's the sort of attitude that will pay off for all of us?"

When you occupy the sales manager's chair you may, at times, be tempted to wear "blinders." Don't do it. Remove your dark glasses and let the light in. Shed light on your common problems. Invite criticism from the men. Get them to let down their hair now and then. Let them get the gripes out of their systems. They may spill more usable information in a half hour's griping session than in a long-winded back-slapping session. It's somewhat like Oscar Wilde saw it: "It is criticism that makes the mind a fine instrument . . . . It takes the cumbersome mass of creative work and distils it into a finer essence."

Criticism from his staff provides the sales manager with a new spring board for measuring his sales leadership power. It's another tool for the sales manager who has mastered the art of persuasion.

The Art of Injecting Persuasion into Objective Planning

Recently I sat down to chat with an unusual sales manager. His men had told me that he was a planning genius. One of his salesmen said: "He sees everything you can imagine popping up in the future. He drives us to get all set to cash in on opportunities which he says are bound to pop up.

Strange thing, too, a lot of things have a way of swinging around to fit right into his plans."

As this enthusiastic young salesman spoke about his sales manager I recalled these lines written by Alfred Lord Tennyson: "For I dipt into the future, far as human eye could see, saw the vision of the world and all the wonders that could be." Today's sales managers might try through constructive and creative planning to peer into the future as Tennyson did.

The sales manager with whom I was chatting did, in fact, dip into the future several times. He saw a *"vision of the . . . wonders that could be."* He had a passion for inspiring salesmen to greatness. This man built sales volume by imaginative, objective planning. He drew heavily on the power of persuasion to stir up his men to increase sales. He drew heavily on the power of persuasion when he taught them, when he gave them guidance, when he issued orders to them. By injecting the art of persuasion into his objective planning this sales manager transmitted his own enthusiasm to his staff.

Successful sales management relies on skillful planning. In some respects the position of sales manager is an exalted spot. It goes beyond salesmanship per se. It even goes beyond sound administration. It goes beyond being a meticulous detail man. Sales management thrives on persuasive ability. It incorporates many virtues which generate the achievement spirit in salesmen. The sales manager who can light within each of his salesmen a fire which flames up, giving to him vision and an awareness of his capacity to achieve, has mastered the art of persuasion. The "miracle power" which ignites such fires is none other than this gentle art.

The following five points are among many which have been found to be success factors for sales managers.

1. Time.
2. Goals.
3. Evaluation and Re-evaluation.
4. Knowledge.
5. Conviction.

Time is your major asset as a sales manager. Time is also the major asset of each of your salesmen. You and each of your salesmen have an equal share of the time supply. Being an executive gives you no edge. Time is a gift to you and to them. However, through your management influence your salesmen can learn how to conserve time. They can learn how to capitalize on time. You and each of your salesmen can learn how to plan better ways and more effective means of putting an end to time-waste. By stopping time-waste each allotted minute can be more productive and consequently individually profitable.

Let's get cold-blooded about fiddling away time. Let's open our eyes to the value of those fleeting minutes by which we can either forge ahead or fall flat. The secrets of all the great achievements in history are wrapped up in minutes. Why should we not salute those 60-second gold nuggets?

To boil the time element down to money let us set the earning capacity of each of your 20 salesmen at $100 a day—an easy-to-work-with figure. That amounts to $500 for a five-day week. We assume that each salesman is on the job eight hours a day, 40 hours a week. This checks out to $12.50 an hour. (Your plumber probably charges you more than that, but for our purposes here we will stand on $100 a day.)

Your salesman gets off to a late start in the morning. He lingers over his mid-morning coffee. He stretches his lunch break. He gets into a long-winded gab session at his mid-afternoon coffee break. He winds up with two hours of non-productive time "lost" from the eight hours of supposed working time.

Now let's move over to your desk—the sales manager's spot. How about your time? We'll modestly set your time worth at $200 a day. This jacks up your hour-value to $25. We'll assume you have contracted some of the same habits as your salesmen. Consequently we'll charge you with two hours of "lost" time daily. You came to work this morning without a constructive plan for the day. This slowed you down. So, you went to the coffee shop to think it over. You also stretched your noon snack-time to an hour and a half. Or, perhaps two hours. You also did a certain amount of non-productive fiddling in your private office, because you hadn't planned that day's work. By the end of the day you, too, "lost" time. But, we'll be considerate and conservative. We'll leave your "lost" time at two hours daily.

None of this is unusual. This sort of time-wasting goes on in your organization and in your competitor's organization. It does, however, point out that we do have too little regard for the golden nugget called a minute. This time-wasting, with its dollar loss, can be cut down to a minimum if we launch a serious time-conservation campaign. We might begin with you. We could then move into the sales force. The idea has been "sold" by others and it can be "sold" by you to your salesmen. It requires, of course, the art of persuasion to give such a campaign enough impact to make it successful.

Goals put guts into objective planning. Sales managers who constantly ring up enviable sales records set up specific goals to shoot for.

One sales manager requires his salesmen to set up and submit to him a copy of their individual goals. He constantly reminds those salesmen of the goals they set for themselves and how well they are doing in the race. This makes each salesman his own motivator. It also demonstrates the flexibility and motivating power in the art of persuasion.

Evaluation and Re-evaluation follow naturally when you and your salesmen have combined your creative strength to plan constructively. When you and also your salesmen have set up achievable goals you have activated objective planning. You get dividends from this by frequent evaluation and re-evaluation. Your goals, your plans to achieve those goals, and your progress come under scrutiny by you and by your salesmen. Do you see how the power of persuasion "works miracles" behind the whole scheme?

Knowledge of your market and of the capacities and problems of your sales staff adds to your strength as a sales manager. To enjoy maximum yield from your market you must know that market. Likewise, to stimulate maximum selling power in your staff you must know your people. By activating the lines of communication between you and your sales force in the field you can reap a harvest of invaluable knowledge for your profit as a sales manager. Motivate and persuade your sales force to keep you advised of the slightest change in the market situation in the territory. This stimulates their powers of observation and adds to their individual selling power. You see, the art of persuasion has many angles by which sales managers can profit.

Conviction is the final test in sound objective planning. Objective and convincing plans incorporate within them something that is persuasive. You may be convinced of the productive power in your plans. Because of this conviction these plans inspire you to take action. That's self-persuasion. Your well-conceived project becomes a passion with you. You infect your staff with the "fever" that has taken possession of you. They respond to your enthusiasm because they can see that they, too, can profit by your plan. Now you have a selling team, all fired up, and driving ahead toward a common goal. This is the mass effect of the art of persuasion in action.

Examining the records of scores of successes in sales management we find these points in evidence relating to the art of persuasion for sales managers:

Those who score high as sales managers lead their salesmen instead of shoving them. This is persuasion.

Those who score high as sales managers display depth of perception and depth of knowledge. This adds to their persuasive power.

Those who score high are skillful, objective planners with persuasive power involved in their plans.

Those who score high as sales managers are persuasive men. Their goals have persuasive qualities. They influence others. They motivate their salesmen to achieve more for their sake.

Such qualities can be acquired. The art of persuasion can be mastered. This art has dynamic power in selling. This art has dynamic power in sales management.

By injecting persuasion into objective planning you feed your plans with dynamic power. Those who score high as sales managers demonstrate the truth of this principle.

Problem-Solving Made Easier by Persuasion

Problem-solving leads you and other sales managers directly to the heart of persuasive power. Without problems there would be little reason for sales managers. Problems are your daily fare. Solving them is your challenge.

As a sales manager and problem-solver you might profit by taking a leaf from Admiral William F. Halsey's note book: "All problems . . . become smaller if you don't dodge them," said Halsey. "Touch a thistle timidly, and it pricks you; grasp it boldly and its spine crumbles. Carry the battle to the enemy; lay your ship alongside his."

Good advice for a sales manager? Let us see. Let us first examine the fundamental power that has been jammed into the art of persuasive selling. It is the power to solve problems. It is the power to sell. Consider these five purposes of the art of persuasion:

1. To Convince.
2. To Influence.
3. To Induce.
4. To Make Willing.
5. To Win Over.

Generally speaking these five, in some way, are involved in the problems which confront sales managers. A sales manager's problems are mainly concerned with people:

People include the salesmen on the staff of the sales manager.

People include the executives who control high level policy for the sales manager.

People are those who buy or should be buying the products or services which the sales manager is charged with selling.

These people initiate and complicate many of your problems. You may already be quite aware that thoughts of *people* disturb your sleep. *People* also make your days less tranquil. Yet, *people* make it possible for you to progress and enjoy the fruits of your creative and persuasive power. *People* are the substance out of which sales records are built. You wonder if what Robert Burns said may apply to the troubled sales manager:

"Good Lord, what is man! . . . All in all, he's a problem must puzzle the devil."

A sales manager for a nation-wide development enterprise told me this: "What I search for in men who come to me aspiring to become salesmen is resourcefulness. If a man is resourceful he will sell. Resourceful men are convincing men. They have influence over others. They can induce others to go along with them. Others respond to them willingly. Such persuasive men win over others. Such resourceful men make the dreams of sales managers realistic."

This sales manager believes, as Admiral Halsey did, that all problems become smaller if he meets them head-on. He did just that with constructive results. His firm was not always big. When he started out with that enterprise he encountered tough competition. His sales problems were compounded. When he found a good man the competition would lure him away. When he closed a substantial deal competition threw up road blocks to delay further expansion. By critical self-examination and re-evaluation of his major problems this sales manager confirmed that *people* were his major problem. His solution: More resourcefulness, combined with greater persuasive power all along the line.

He got busy. He began with himself. He re-examined his strategy, his attitudes, his persuasive power. He then came up with this formula for problem-solving:

(a) *Define the problem.* Break it down into small units.

(b) *Define the objectives.*

(c) *Map out a constructive approach to solve the problem.*

(d) *Use selling strategy all the way.* Basically you are a salesman.

(e) *Make a frontal attack on the problem.* Plan your attack well. Go in well-armed. Go in with product knowledge, with market knowledge, with resourcefulness. And, gather around you resourceful salesmen.

(f) *Reinforce the whole operation with the total power in the art of persuasion for sales managers.*

Mastery of the art of persuasion convinces even the most skeptical sales managers that problems are strength-builders. Men grow in stature by solving problems. Problems can be converted into incentives for increasing sales. Problems can also uncover incentives for buying. Resourceful salesmanship, backed up by resourceful sales managers, has demonstrated that these goals can be achieved through the art of persuasion.

Sales managers who profit most by problem-solving ask such questions as these:

Which one of my men can contribute most to solving this problem? (By making this decision another persuasive factor is added to the sales manager's persuasive power structure.)

Is my problem real, or have I been harboring a notion? (Further examination in depth and investigation of all facets of the problem may open the way for persuasive action.)

Is this problem mine, or the problem of my staff, or the problem of my firm? (Again re-examination should unveil the realistic aspects of your problem.)

Why am I saddled with this problem?

If you have 50 salesmen on your staff you have 50 problems, plus you, making a total of 51 problems. These problems should encourage you to evolve an objective attitude toward problems. The personal problems of your salesmen ultimately will, in some way, become your problems. These, too, challenge your persuasive power.

This is a realistic view of your very realistic position as a sales manager. Problems which disturb you must be thought-provoking. Otherwise they would not disturb you. From this, then, you can find much to encourage you as a sales manager. Even much to motivate you. As a creative, persuasive sales manager, resourceful and with leadership ability, you contrive, you invent, you figure out ways and means to gain your ends. Problems and problem-solving stimulate your thinking. Such stimulation can become highly profitable to you, as it has for so many other sales managers. You might get some encouragement from what Goethe, the German philosopher, said about thinking: "Everything has been thought of before, but the difficulty is to think of it again."

Problem-solving becomes easier when you refuse to allow problems to intimidate you, when you attack those problems with resourcefulness and your full persuasive power.

How to Firm Up Leadership by Persuasion

The art of persuasion strengthens leadership. This has been demonstrated in virtually every field of activity. In selling, those leaders who inspire and motivate their sales staffs are persuasive sales managers. Their persuasive power results in moving the world's goods from producers to ultimate consumers. It is the motivating power that keeps commerce in high gear.

Previously this point has been made: That sales management and the art of persuasion are so closely linked that they might be considered as twins.

Likewise sales management and leadership have identical implications. I have met no successful sales managers who were devoid of leadership qualities. Examination of case records of outstanding sales successes provides convincing evidence that mastery of the art of persuasion strengthens leadership qualities in sales managers as it does in the salesmen they direct. Those who master this art transmit its influence to others. By persuasion they lead others to respond to their will. This, of course, is effective selling. This is also effective leadership. It can, and does, result in dynamic sales management.

One sales manager in the highly competitive detergent industry related this situation: "My figures indicated that only 12% of the time of my salesmen was actually devoted to selling. Reports from other sources indicated that my figures were favorable. Those reports cut down selling time to 10%. But, I'm not satisfied with 12% now, nor was I then. I wanted and intended to get more than seven or eight minutes of selling time out of an hour."

In 60 days after making this statement this sales manager scored a sales gain and he was still dissatisfied. He was unconvinced that this gain had resulted from more productive selling time. Six months later his figures indicated his salesmen were putting in about 18 minutes of face-to-face selling in each hour on the job. This represented a gain of 50% over that low 12% which had annoyed him.

Now another reverse developed, complicating this sales manager's over-all problem. Total sales dropped in spite of an increase in selling time. Again he went out in search of the cause of this imbalance. This is what he learned:

1. Salesmen were spending too much time on paper work and other desk chores.
2. Salesmen were spending too much time traveling to and returning from contacts assigned to them.
3. Salesmen were spending too much time waiting to get in to buyers and prospects.

Critical self-examination disclosed that this sales manager was responsible for loading his salesmen with paper work. He had introduced three new forms in the past month. He decided to re-evaluate these forms.

By observation this sales manager discovered that salesmen were developing "executive syndrome." They enjoyed lingering at their desks instead of getting out to their prospective buyers.

Further critical self-examination fixed the blame for lost time due to salesmen traveling to and returning from assigned prospects or customers. These assignments were made from the sales manager's office. This was one situation which he exposed:

Salesman "A" was in the immediate area on the day Salesman "B" was sent out on a special trip to see a prospect. This sales manager also learned that Salesman "A" and Salesman "B" met that day and discussed at length the "blunders of the front office." This, too was "time out" from selling. So, the cause of lost selling-time in this instance was shared by the sales manager's office and by the two salesmen.

Selling time lost by salesmen in "cooling their heels" had been put on the unsolvable list until he examined the problem more thoroughly. He then persuaded his salesmen to do more appointment selling, use the phone more, and cut down on waiting time. He and his salesmen discovered that buyers and prospects generally liked the appointment system better than having salesmen crash in at an inopportune moment. As appointment selling gained, selling time increased and sales went up for this sales manager.

In attempting to solve the lost-selling-time problem in three areas, the art of persuasion became directly involved in the solutions:

1. This sales manager graphically showed his staff how much selling time they had lost and how much this lost time had cost each of them. This hit home. By persuasive leadership this sales manager got constructive action.
2. This sales manager demonstrated how time could be found to get out reports without losing prime selling time. He presented plans for time-budgeting and call-planning, which could result in increasing income for the salesmen. Again this sales manager became a creative, understanding, persuasive leader of men.

Because this sales manager had drawn heavily on the art of persuasion his sales staff achieved two things: (a) increased average selling time; (b) increased sales.

We asked this sales manager why his first step-up in active selling time resulted in a slump in sales. He replied:

"Simple. My figures were cockeyed. My men were crediting waiting time to selling time. Some were also crediting report and order writing to selling time. But, even with cockeyed figures we made progress. Those figures jarred us into getting down to the hard facts in this business.

Things aren't always as they seem to be on the surface. You have to dig down deep."

By tackling a problem head-on, digging out the reasons for lost sales, finding a solution to the problem, and promoting better team work in his staff this sales manager demonstrated that there is "miracle power" in the art of persuasion.

By drawing on this same "miracle power" you, too, can firm up your effectiveness as a leader, raise your status as an executive, and produce more abundant sales—if you master the art of persuasion.

chapter 3

How to Pry Open Manager-Salesman Communication Channels by Persuasion

This is your problem: Communication channels between you and your salesmen have suddenly become plugged up.

This is your solution: Pry open those plugged up communication channels. Restore communication between you and your salesmen "for sales sake."

"Too simple," did you say? Not at all.

When communication lines between you and your staff break down you work in a sort of vacuum. You grope around in the dark. You wonder why your last directives to your sales staff stirred up no enthusiasm and were disappointing in results. You wonder why sales in this and that area have fallen down. You also wonder why some other area shows a gain. You are in the dark. You are unable to pinpoint the reason for either success or failure. Now a ray of light penetrates the fog. You see why these things are happening without your knowledge. Your communication channels are plugged up. Information is not getting back to you from the field force.

Tragically, your salesmen are in the same boat with you. They feel the loss of communication. With communication lines down they feel they are far, far away from home base. They also grope around in the dark. Of course they get out and make calls every day. They skim off the easy-to-get business. This keeps the wolf from howling too loudly at their doors. But they are somewhat of the same mind as you. They want more out of life than they are getting. Basically they want their work to be more profitable for them. So, with communication channels plugged up between them and their sales manager they become uneasy and dissatisfied. They become victims of the "what's the use" attitude and this rebounds to penalize you, the sales manager. Their drive is gone. This must be restored. Communication must be restored.

Plugged up communication lines are a threat to effective sales management. A communication blackout allows blunders to go unnoticed or to be concealed. A communication blackout permits notable sales achievements in the field to go unnoticed. Plugged up communication lines slow down business all along the line.

What to do about it? Those plugged up communication lines between you and your sales staff must be pried open, and quickly. Your status as the "sales boss" is at stake. Or maybe it's the "boss image" that has contributed to plugging up the communication lines. Perhaps the image needs to be changed to the "chief image" or something else more palatable to those in the field going after business. Take heart, however, you do not stand alone at this critical point. The status of every salesman on your staff is involved. When he lets down his pride slips. He must keep his head up, feed his family, keep his bank account out of the red. Breakdown in communication has raised hob with his enthusiasm. Now his enthusiasm must be restored. This gets back to you, his sales manager.

It's up to you to unplug those plugged up communication lines and *this can be done.* Case records reveal how it has been done. You have an effective "miracle tool" for prying open plugged up communication lines. That tool is the art of persuasion. Let us look into some of the principles involved in prying open manager-salesman communication channels.

Grab Their Attention to Activate Persuasion

The simple truth about opening communication channels, or reopening them, is this: *It's a selling job!*

A salesman's first objective is to get attention. The sales manager, striving to restore communication, bids for the attention of his salesmen. He has a message. He wants to get it across. In effect, this is what he wants to accomplish: "Now you listen to me." But, being a man of executive wisdom he takes another approach. He moves in persuasively to grab the attention of his salesmen.

Four methods of grabbing attention are effective. They have been tested in a variety of problem-solving situations. When your communication channels get plugged up try these four unplugging methods:

1. The Direct Question Method.
2. The Dramatic Method.
3. The Appeal to Self-Interest Method.
4. The Always-Be-Interesting Method.

The direct question method, persuasively used, takes salesmen into your confidence. You make them part of the picture. You seek their ideas on how things could be improved. If they prosper, you prosper. You draw them out on how they would suggest going about stepping up the overall sales volume. You invite their suggestions on how the sales manager can be helpful to them in reaching their selling goals. You invite their ideas on how their own selling methods can be improved, and what you can contribute to this. Doing this you take them into the team. You unplug that channel of communication which may have been the cause of creating an idea that the home office, which you represent, has no interest in the individual problems of salesmen. By unplugging communication lines you can squash that notion of no interest in your staff. This, then, is the persuasive approach. You put the art of persuasion to work for you. It is the power tool for dynamic sales managers.

Drama, too, has a definite place in the sales manager's persuasive power. Dramatic presentations are potent attention-arresters. We may not all be capable of presenting a smashing dramatic performance to compete with the cinema or TV. But, we can arrange for or present our ideas in such a way that the salesmen, whom we are trying to influence, will say: "Gee, I'll buy that. I can cash in on that deal."

The startling development of a new product suggests an announcement with dramatic impact.

The case record of how a difficult sale was wrapped up suggests the possibility of a dramatic demonstration by the salesman involved.

Dramatic methods of grabbing attention to activate persuasion require: (a) enthusiasm on the part of the one making the presentation; (b) supporting visual aids such as films, slides, charts, etc.; (c) the product itself, in action, if appropriate.

Sales managers who dig out dramatic possibilities find a rich source of ways to keep channels of communication open between them and their salesmen. Dramatic effect, in itself, has persuasive power.

When a sales manager talks to a salesman about "How *you* can profit" he's getting mighty persuasive. Self-interest usually gets attention. Show anyone how to benefit and you activate persuasion.

A sales manager in the toy business utilized the direct question method, the dramatic method, and the appeal to self-interest method to stir up his sales staff to make the territory each of them covered a veritable toy land. He was a persuasive, enthusiastic man. He kept his communication channels open by creating the impression that he was devoted to making life more profitable for each of his salesmen, which he was. They responded because they were just as selfish about it as he was. They liked their "chief." He had convinced them that he was doing great things for them, because he was sincere about it. Human nature reacts that way.

Self-interest appeals are in order in almost every phase of moving goods and services:

An authentic story of how someone else cashed in rouses self-interest. It is persuasive. It suggests, "go and do likewise."

A detailed market study can be made persuasive. Show how the market change affects each salesman. Show them how they can benefit by the shifting market.

Even blunders made by your salesmen can be so presented that they will not offend or embarrass. Those blunders can be inspiring. Show how the blunder was made. Show how it could have been avoided. Show how a neat profit could have resulted from a different approach. Show that the blunder was not final. Show how the way is still open to turn that blunder into a profitable sale. Play up the benefit possibilities in blunders. Play down the loss.

Elbert Hubbard had a word for those who take the sour view of a situation rather than looking at it through rose-colored glasses. He said: "The world is moving so fast these days that the man who says it can't be done generally is interrupted by someone doing it."

Building the confidence of men is a challenge to your persuasive power as a sales manager. It is vital if a man has made a blunder. It keeps communication channels open.

A top ranking industrial executive expressed high regard for "making everything interesting." He laid down this principle: "If there is no interest in the matter, why bring it up? Dullness is inexcusable. The matter you are about to present to your people may be vital, and yet you contend that it is drab. This cannot be. If you'll dig deep enough you may discover something of transcendant interest in it. If this isn't true, why is it so vital?"

The always-be-interesting method of grabbing attention can be a powerful force for sales managers. It activates persuasion. It influences others to come around to your way of thinking in order to produce greater sales volume.

The Persuasive Manner: Tell It to 'Em Straight

When you tell it to them straight you pry open manager-salesman communication channels. The average salesman backs up, squints his skeptical eyes, and goes on the defensive if you shower him with a blast of meaningless words. If you tell it to him straight you get his attention, create interest, and you probably will get him to do something about it. This is true whether you have good news or bad news for him.

As a sales manager you have three standard methods of communicating with your sales staff:

1. Writing.
2. Phoning.
3. Face-to-Face.

The short, crisp, meaningful memo usually is the one that gets attention. A memo never was intended to be a medium for putting across a sermon or a formal address. The short, crisp, meaningful memo with a personal touch has tremendous persuasive power.

A sales director in the clothing industry made single words do a persuasive communication job for him on favorable sales reports from his salesmen. We went through a stack of sales reports in quick time. In the upper right-hand corner of each report he wrote just one word and initialed it. Such single words as "improving," "great," "excellent," "commendable," "progress," all had impact—persuasive impact.

Unfavorable reports got brief notations, too. Seldom were these held to a single word. They were helpful, however. His initaled notations on less favorable reports were along this line: "See me." "How can this be improved?" "How do we go about getting more of this customer's business?" Note how persuasiveness took the sting out of these crisp remarks.

The phone is not the place for a long-winded discussion. A phone call from the sales manager to a salesman is intended to get action. If it is to the point, pleasant, and persuasive it will probably gain its objective.

As a sales manager you make phone calls to salesmen primarily to get business. Your salesman isn't going to accomplish much that day if you anger him and leave him with a dead receiver in his hand. But if you have encouraged him, inspired him, fired him up to release his full persuasive power on prospective accounts he is going to go after new business. And, after all, isn't that the reason sales managers should make telephone calls? Or do some of us make phone calls in a fit of anger? If we do we may kill some salesman's enthusiasm. We may slow him down, instead of refueling him. We may put him in a mood to strike out each time he goes to bat that day with a prospective buyer. Sour phone calls have a curdling effect. The pleasant, upbeat phone call is persuasive. It stirs up persuasive power which results in sales.

As a sales manager you may succeed in hiding your emotions behind a memo pad. You may be able to control the pitch of your voice on the phone. Comes the moment, however, in a face-to-face confrontation with your salesmen when you have to get your point across. This is the moment when you tell it to them straight. You do this to be understood, to be convincing and to be persuasive. You tell it to them straight to get definite results.

A rather modest, yet effective, sales manager in the industrial field, made this confession to his staff one morning: "I have a strange idea that your personal problems and your problems on the job are my problems, too. I want to help you solve them, if I can. I want to see each of you get a bigger pay check next month than I get. That can be possible, you understand. To accomplish this I have some strange ideas about what you can do to make all this come about. I believe that every sales pitch you make must have the ring of importance. If what you are selling doesn't seem to be important to you, if it's just so-so, I can't see how you can make it seem important to your prospects. I believe that your personality should blend favorably with the personality of the house you represent. I believe that you and I should maintain standards that will make us stand out from the ordinary run of guys in our line of business. I believe that we have here an outstanding group of salesmen. I believe that we represent an outstanding firm. I have a notion that we can profit by talking about this favorable point more than we have been doing. Our customers and prospective customers are entitled to know what we think about the people we work for. Let's sell them on this house. Doing that we will be selling them on ourselves. Let's tell it to them straight.

"I believe you get the point. I have made a sort of confession, an admission, and I have given it to you straight, telling you what I believe. My sole purpose in doing this is to encourage you to go out each day with one big purpose in your mind—to *sell.* We have no other reason for being in this business."

What did this sales manager accomplish by telling it to them straight? Just this: Sales volume picked up in the weeks that followed.

Did this, then, solve his problem and attain his objective? Of course not. Persuasive effort is a continuing process. This sales manager, seeing that one persuasive effort brought favorable results, was now enthusiastic about creating another persuasive appeal.

He realized that he had to set up other goals with profit potentials and he would have to sell these goals to his staff.

He realized that he would have to devise new and more appealing selling plans and that he would have to sell these plans to his staff.

He realized that he had only begun to advance toward his own personal goals. He had witnessed the power of persuasion in action.

This sales manager had captured the interest of his salesmen. He had won their confidence. He had stirred them up. He had seen new enthusiasm in their attitude. He had done this by "telling it to 'em straight." He had also convinced himself that persuasion is a potent force for sales managers to use.

Five Effective Steps to Persuasive Communication

From the moment the alarm clock jars a salesman out of bed in the morning until he snaps off the TV after the late-late show a salesman is directly involved in communication. If he is to be successful this communication must, in the main, be persuasive, because he will be endeavoring to influence others to see things his way.

The lot of the sales manager is similar to that of the salesman. During his waking hours the sales manager also is involved in communication. If he is to be a successful, productive sales manager, communication with his salesmen must be persuasive. He will be working on them, and with them. He will be exerting his influence to persuade them to become more productive salesmen.

There are five effective steps to such persuasive communication. There may be other steps but these five will get you there in productive order. These five steps have been used by sales managers in many highly competitive fields of selling. They have been used by executives in virtually every industry. They have also been used by editors, teachers, and even by military commanders. These five steps are simple, yet they are effective. Perhaps it is because they are so simple that many of us give them only passing thought. Let's take a moment out of our jittery day and look into the wisdom of these five steps in *persuasive communication:*

1. *Be specific.* (Vagueness cools interest, lacks persuasive power.)
2. *Come down out of the clouds—get down to earth.* (Talking

down to others also cools interest. It also lacks persuasive power.)

3. *Speak clearly—be understood—maintain your composure.* (Use the short word. Be brief, but not pompous. Speak to your listeners, not over them. Avoid anger. Handle criticism and disruptions calmly.)

4. *Promptly clarify misunderstanding.* (If you're wrong, admit it. If you're not understood, hang on until you are understood.)

5. *Maintain enthusiasm.* (This is your most valuable asset as a sales manager. Cling to your enthusiasm. Nourish it. It's the most contagious fever a sales manager can contract. Salesmen catch this fever and break down sales barriers with it. Enthusiasm is the heart and soul of the art of persuasion.)

The specific is usually more persuasive than the general. In sales manager's jargon "merchandise" can mean almost anything. But "shoes," that's different. The word "shoes" stirs up in the minds of salespeople thoughts of styles, of colors, of price ranges, of competitive lines. So it is with "watches" rather than "jewelry;" or with "typewriter," or "computer" rather than speaking about "business machines." The specific creates mental pictures. The specific is more clearly understood. It is also more persuasive.

One sales manager became irritable because selling errors were resulting in lost sales. Another sales manager, faced with the same problem, got down to brass tacks with his salesmen. He stipulated each error. He explained how and why each error had resulted in loss of business. He admitted that he had committed the same errors and had suffered the same losses as a salesman. He pulled each error apart. He showed his men how easy it was to get into the habit of making such errors. His was the specific approach. He spoke of the results of errors and became specific about those results. He was persuasive. He influenced his salesmen to strive to avoid errors. This was his objective.

Fairfax Cone, internationally known advertising and marketing executive, once made this point: "It is the primary requirement of advertising to be clear." That seems to be right on target for salesmanship, too. That's understandable because advertising is also salesmanship relying on another form of communication. The primary requirement of effective sales management is also to be clear.

Those who are in sales management spots as well as those who are in the field making direct contacts with buyers and potential buyers develop the "up, up, up syndrome." This affliction takes us off into space.

We go into orbit over our buyers and prospective buyers. We hover over the heads of our sales force. We lose communication with our salesmen. We are fortunate, therefore, when someone takes direct action and kicks us out of the clouds.

When we get down to earth we discover how insignificant we really are. We discover that those other people are pretty much on a par with us. When this light dawns we come down to a more persuasive level. We begin to sell again. We begin to put across our ideas. Our salesmen begin to believe in us. We begin to enjoy the thrill of having others want to do what we want them to do. We accomplish this through the art of persuasion.

Misunderstandings clear up much easier when we communicate on the same level. Arguments we avoid. Discussions we encourage.

Having taken the five steps to persuasive communication you can now fortify your persuasive strength by using these five keys for prying open manager-salesmen communication channels:

1. *To your sales staff,* clearly and objectively present your problems or your proposal with your objective.
2. *To your sales staff,* clearly and objectively explain how the problem affects them. Explain how your proposal can benefit them. Explain how, collectively, the problem can be solved. Explain how the salesmen can profit by such team work. Get them to "buy" your proposal.
3. *On the downbeat,* show your staff how and where salesmen have lost sales. Indicate specifically where and how these losses have been suffered. Point out clearly and specifically how each salesman directly involved in these errors lost sales and dollars. Present a clear picture of total dollar losses from sales oversights. Show your salesmen how to recapture those sales or those losses. Show them how they can individually profit by doing it right.
4. *On the upbeat,* glorify exceptional sales achievements of members of your staff. Show where, how and why sales successes have been scored so all may profit by the case record. Make a point of how much individual earnings are increased by such sales successes. Point out to the staff how they become involved and benefit when overall sales go up.
5. *Set up goals* and make goals realistic. Make them high enough to be challenging. Make them low enough to be attainable. Demonstrate how and explain why sales gains can be made to the individual profit of each salesman. Be

specific. Your staff will enjoy this direct fire. They will accept it. They will profit by it. Attainable goals, backed up by case records to show that it can be done, are loaded with dynamic persuasive power.

How to Tune in by Persuasion on Group Conferences

At this point we are interested in the so-called group conference. This is quite different from the sales conference. The group conference is a catch-all for problems, policies, and ideas. It may be called with no advance notice.

A sales manager's motive for calling a group conference may be problems relating to company policy. It may involve clarification of management viewpoint. Such situations require "salesmanship" to present the subject in a favorable light to favorably impress the sales staff. To accomplish this purpose the sales manager "tunes in" on his group conference through his persuasive power.

The group conference which is concerned chiefly with the sales manager's problems and objectives has a character all its own. Without an agenda the sales manager is on his own. This presents both an advantage and a hazard. With no agenda the sales manager has more latitude in conducting his conference. He is also confronted with the hazard of the conference getting out of his control. To maintain control the sales manager faces this three-point challenge:

1. *To tune in when he raps the gavel.* At that precise moment he does something to capture mass interest.
2. *To remain tuned in.* Fire up interest of the group. Dramatize the reasons for calling the conference. Make it important. Specify how and why each salesman is affected by the subject under discussion. Suggest what to do about it.
3. *To sign off with mass approval of the "big idea."* A group conference which adjourns on a high note of mass enthusiasm can be chalked up as a success.

One sales manager who achieved sales increases against oppressive odds made the art of persuasion pay off for him in group conferences. His men called him "The Riddle." He kept them guessing. His conference calls stirred up interest. "What's he up to now?" was the dominant question.

This sales manager won his sobriquet by often cramming his conferences with shocking examples of how sales were lost, how competition had slipped in and made off with what he called "substantial loot" of what he contended should have been their business. He was helpful, however. He was thought-provoking. He was as lavish with praise as he was with biting criticism. In either instance this sales manager was persuasive.

"The Riddle" once said: "I can think of nothing more dismal for salesmen to behold than their sales manager stumbling to the podium with a stack of papers in his arms. To a salesman a stack of papers suggests one thing: A boring session. I know of no better way to kill a conference. So, I hide my papers. When I need some of them I yell at my secretary. She digs them out. That's different from me standing before the group shuffling papers. The salesmen aren't bored by my secretary digging out papers. But, let me do it, and I've lost them.

"I try to get interest into my conferences. I usually trot in instead of walking. I force a smile even if I'm burning up. I've even tried clowning to keep my salesmen on their toes. Anything goes in my conferences to get results. I go after their interest. When I get it I hang on. It's the vehicle that will carry me to where I want to go. First, *interest.* Then *understanding.* Finally, *acceptance."*

Impromptu conferences—those quickie group conferences—can become highly productive. Out of such quickie sessions have come great ideas. Seeds have been planted which have sprouted into high sales volume. Morale has been boosted in spirited group conferences. To achieve such results in so-called group conferences two things are required:

1. *An idea loaded with explosive selling power.*
2. *Dynamic presentation* to stir up the sales staff; to create desire to get to the nearest prospect at once and to sell the idea that has been presented.

The secret of tuning in on group conferences is the same secret which has created sales giants and dynamic sales managers—*the art of persuasion.* This is the art of influencing others. This is the "miracle power" that gets results by "tuning in," staying "tuned in" and getting across this message:

"Let me show you how you can benefit if you do as I suggest and put to use what I have to sell—a dynamic, persuasive idea."

Getting Through to the Individual by Persuasion

As sales manager you have as many barriers to cross in "getting through" to your salesmen as you have salesmen on your staff. Each of those men (or women) is a distinctive individual who projects to you a challenge to "get through" to him (or her). You can't afford to have a communication gap.

In effect, you are in the same boat as your salesmen, with this exception: They are dealing with prospective buyers. You are dealing with salesmen, who are your prospective "buyers." You are asking them to "buy" your ideas or whatever it is that you are trying to get across to them.

To assist you in "getting through" to your salesmen here is a five-step plan which other executives have found to be effective:

1. Step into your salesman's shoes. Try to see things through his eyes. Try to assume his position. Try to visualize and understand his problems in selling. Speak to him in his language.

2. Convince the salesman of your personal interest in him. Persuade him to feel that what you want him to accomplish was his idea all along.

3. Challenge your salesman. Set up an attainable goal for him. Convince him that you do sincerely believe that he has the capacity to attain that goal. Sell him on the idea of his own capacity to achieve more than he is achieving.

4. Get your salesman excited about his product and his job. Dramatize your idea. Draw your salesman into the act. After all you want him to be the "star" in this performance.

5. Get close to your salesman. Reach out to him. Allow him to feel your personal warmth. Invite him to become an important factor in your selling team. Hammer away on what this program you have in mind can mean to him in personal fortune. Build him up. Don't talk down to him.

What is it we are trying to do here? We are striving to close any communication gap that may exist between you and your salesman. We are also trying to increase that salesman's production. (Note that this is in the singular.) Each salesman on your staff is a distinctive individual. To get through to him you must take an individual, personal approach. We are striving to communicate persuasively with that salesman. We are striving to transmit an idea to him. We are trying to impress him with the importance to him of that idea. We can do this by personal contact, by voice (including phone calls), or by writing.

The surest way to effectively communicate with this salesman is to make our proposal (a) simple; (b) clear; (c) interesting; (d) understandable; (e) appealing.

The principle involved in "getting through" to the individual is to release your full persuasive power upon him. This involves inducing him to see things your way. It involves simplicity. It involves clarity and interest. With these elements what you have to present becomes understandable.

With these elements what you have to propose becomes more appealing. In substance, your presentation thereby becomes more persuasive.

Persuasion is the "miracle power" that will enable you to "get through" to the individual salesman. It will enable you to close the communication gap. This is the same "miracle power" that enables you to get favorable mass reaction in your group conferences. The art of persuasion is the "miracle power" of dynamic sales management.

chapter 4

How to Build a
Persuasive Sales Staff

An industrial executive once remarked that sales management must never be permitted to become an "honorary" position.

"Sales management," said he, "is the vehicle on which commerce rides, either to get somewhere or to crack up. The sales manager is the pilot of this vehicle. He's in the driver's seat. He's the fellow we hold accountable for selling our products. We expect him to search out, to screen, to select men of talent for his selling team. We expect him to train those men, and to motivate them, and to equip them to get around road blocks and keep the sales vehicle going in high gear."

Three challenges become the companions of sales managers when they step into the "driver's seat." These three challenges cling to those sales managers, at times troubling them, at times haunting them, at other times inspiring them and motivating them. This, then, is the challenging trio, troublesome, yet helpful:

1. *People*—Search for selling talent. Screen this talent, separating mediocrity from superiority.
2. *Training*—Detailed orientation. Illuminating the overall business policy of your firm so it becomes clear to those whom you send out to sell your goods. Developing individual selling skills. Increasing individual persuasive power. Stressing the *work* theme, not the ease theme.
3. *Motivation*—This is the fuel which keeps the "sales vehicle"

running at high gear. Motivation is the product of persuasion.

The sales manager of a chain of automobile dealerships uses two methods of initiating new salesmen into car-selling. "This is where executive judgment of men either pays off or double-crosses you," this sales executive said. "Some new salesmen do well by cold canvassing. Others can't take it. Many of these, however, turn out well dealing with pre-sold prospects. They find such prospects "warm." They succeed in closing them. This may be due to those prospects feeling less pressure from the new salesman than from the hard-driving pro. I try out new salesmen on both methods. In this way I learn about the capabilities of my men. I learn about their weaknesses and their strength."

When a sales manager is searching out selling talent he actually is on a selling assignment himself. In this role he becomes most persuasive if he presents a clear picture of the opportunities he can offer a salesman. One sales manager warns: "Don't make it appear too easy for them. After all, we're out to build hard-working staffs, not leisure clubs."

Orientation calls for top priority in a sales manager's training program. Clear-cut statements of policy are definite aids to selling. Granted, much of house policy comes to light through experience, but a general understanding of how the firm does business is necessary equipment for salesmen.

Motivation? Those you may have selected must have had some reason for seeking employment with you. Find out what that reason is. What motivated them to come to you? Shifting now to the sales manager's viewpoint: What motivated you to encourage those prospective salesmen?

Having answered those two questions your challenge becomes clear. Your objective now is to totally motivate the individuals you finally select to become productive members of your team.

Building a persuasive sales staff is, indeed, a "shirt-sleeve job" having *top executive status.* Sales management in this category searches out, screens, selects, orients, trains and motivates people to buckle down to work as a team and to produce sales volume.

To achieve these objectives requires dynamic sales management, and dynamic sales management is the product of the art of persuasion.

Play on Self-Interest for Greater Persuasive Effect

Today's tip for sales managers:
Read the biblical admonition in Luke 4:23: "Physician heal thyself." Doesn't this suggest that a dose of our own medicine may be in order? We might profit by doing what we have been urging our salesmen to do. For

instance, how about talking to a salesman or to a prospective salesman about how he can make his own position better?

As a starting point, try one or all of the following five appeals on your sales staff. Observe the response. Determine if these five approaches have the desired persuasive appeal you want:

1. Dramatize the possibilities of greater income.
2. Glorify the possibilities of personal advancement.
3. Appeal to their pride to motivate them.
4. Glorify their status in business to motivate them.
5. Make the importance of his spot on your selling team impressive.

To make those five points most persuasive you will strive to know more about your staff. You will learn all you can about each salesman, about his home life, about his hopes, his ambitions, his hobbies, his capacity and willingness to carry a heavy workload.

You will seek ways to motivate each salesman to "tie his talents to a star." Without intimate knowledge and understanding of your sales staff you are handicapped in motivation and persuasion.

A tempting, lucrative piece of business has come to your attention. You desire to add this account to your other accounts. This challenges you. Your problem is this: "Which of my salesmen can get through to that buyer? Which one can influence him and bag that choice account?"

You pick your man to do this job. No sooner done than another question pops up: "Is this the man, once landing the account, who can hold on to that account and develop it for its maximum potential?"

Some time ago a soft-drink trucker-salesman was extolling the goodness of the product he sold. He was stocking shelves in a supermarket with his brand of "pop." The store manager was exchanging pleasantries with him. A shopper suggested to the store manager that he get rid of soft drinks and stock a greater variety of food items. "I never touch soda," he said. The trucker-salesman smiled. "Try this for a drink," he said, uncapping a bottle of his brand of "pop" and holding it out to the shopper. "Never," replied the shopper, "I don't believe it's good for the body."

Calmly the trucker-salesman directed the shopper's attention to the ingredients printed on the label. "Nourishing, refreshing," he assured the shopper. Then he poured out a small drink. "Try this," he suggested. The customer tried it. "Not bad," he said. The trucker-salesman continued to "sell" this shopper on "pop," as a delightful, refreshing beverage. Before that shopper had left the store he had a six-pack in his shopping cart. "First I've ever bought," he chuckled.

Some time later this soda-pop trucker showed up in businessman's attire. He had joined the sales force. The word got back to his sales manager about his selling job with the shopper who had never tasted their "pop."

So far we have concentrated on recruits in the business. What about veteran salesmen? Do they respond to self-interest appeals? You can bet your credit card that they do. Self-interest persuasive power is unrestricted. Nor is it confined to money appeal. It's a matter of communication. A sincere compliment is persuasive. Praise may persuade a salesman to prove that he is a top-flight producer. A deserved compliment for personal appearance, for an idea, for closing a tough deal, for maintaining his "cool" in a tight situation with an unruly customer, all may contain the magic power of persuasion. Self-interest is involved in all of these cases.

Placing responsibility on a man also plays on his self-interest. He's out to prove that you are right, that he will make good.

Coleman Du Pont, industrialist and financier, once laid down this principle: "I believe in placing full responsibility upon the man I select. If a man wants my advice, my judgment, I am ready to give it to him, but I insist that he make the final decision. The action then becomes his, not mine. He is responsible for the outcome, not I." Therein lies the strength of the self-interest appeal in responsibility.

Recognition of a man's meritorious performance appeals to his self-interest. It has a persuasive effect. It motivates him to greater effort. Great and difficult sales have been closed because a sales manager took note of and recognized a lesser victory by a salesman on his staff.

Self-interest involves a man's income, his health, his education, his family, his friends, his household, his hobbies, his talents, his achievements, his aspirations. The more a sales manager knows about these things as they relate to each of his salesmen the nearer he can get to them. By appealing to their self-interests the sales manager can profit and his salesmen can profit, which amounts to persuasion in team work.

Seven Persuasive Qualities to Develop in Salesmen

A far-seeing man who propelled himself from a volume-writing salesman in the tire industry into a district sales manager's chair learned this lesson early in his career:

"The sales manager worth his salt wears many hats," he said. "He becomes a teacher, a philosopher of sorts, a counselor, a trouble-shooter, a whipping boy, and, presumably, a leader of men. In addition, he remains at heart a salesman. Few days pass without his need for persuasive salesmanship. His staff may at times doubt him as well as believe in him. He requires persuasive selling power to put across his ideas. He requires that same persuasive power to motivate his men. Throughout his career as a sales manager he is confronted with this challenge: To maintain the balance in his own favor."

To be a goal-setter is one of the many requirements of an effective sales manager. To achieve this he inspires men to develop qualities which drive them toward established objectives in selling. Seven persuasive qualities in men have contributed to successes in selling. They have been responsible for developing great sales volume. These qualities have boosted individual incomes. These qualities in salesmen have brought stature, progress and financial rewards to their sales managers.

Here are seven persuasive qualities which, when developed in your salesmen, will pay off for those salesmen and also for you as their sales manager who motivated them to succeed:

1. *Perceptiveness* plus an interest in the welfare of prospective customers and in the products those salesmen sell.
2. *Insatiable hunger for knowledge* about people, about markets, about methods, about new and better sales techniques.
3. *Honesty* with no qualifying strings tied to it.
4. *Persuasive leadership* propelled by dynamic persuasive power.
5. *Humility* which is more persuasive than arrogance.
6. *Enthusiasm* energized by full persuasive power.
7. *A sense of humor* which attracts, never repels; builds up, never belittles.

A sales manager's first step in developing such qualities in his salesmen is to detect ability within his sales staff. Elbert Hubbard, successful businessman, author, publisher, and "salesman" of ideas, put it this way: "There is something that is much more sacred, much finer by far than ability. It is the ability to recognize ability."

By developing or teaching salesmen how to develop the foregoing seven persuasive qualities, and how to put those qualities to work for them in the market place, the sales manager motivates his staff to achieve greatness in selling.

Sales managers who also develop within themselves those seven persuasive qualities gain strength of leadership which, case records conclusively prove, can ignite a fire of staff enthusiasm which propels sales volume to new heights.

Persuasive Aids to Evaluating Selling Ability

"Give me 60 minutes with an applicant for a selling position and I will make a reasonable appraisal of his fitness for selling."

That statement was made by a self-confident sales manager with a high score for low turnover on his staff and high sales volume.

"Persuasive aids" for evaluating ability to sell may include skillful tactics which influence others to expose their traits, both negative and positive. When we discover how to influence Mr. Jones to open up and disclose his attitudes on relevant matters related to selling we have found a "persuasive aid" for sound evaluation of Mr. Jones' probable qualifications as a salesman.

Classification of traits has been used and is invaluable as a "persuasive aid" for such evaluations. A man's traits have definite relationship to his prospects for success in selling. Therefore, sales managers are vitally concerned with the traits of their applicants. You may find it desirable to interview a prospective salesman several times under a variety of circumstances. Time is of the essence if you seriously intend to make your talent search satisfying profit-wise.

Classification is a sound starting point for learning what makes your applicant tick. A check list has been found useful and effective by many executives. It is another "persuasive aid" in uncovering positive and negative traits related to selling.

The check list should not be filled in during your interview. To do so would distract your applicant. He might "tighten up" and you would not succeed in getting a satisfactory appraisal. Instead your most valuable "persuasive aid" is to make it easy for your applicant to relax, to feel at ease. Only then will he speak freely.

The following check list is suggestive. It has been used effectively, but you may find it advantageous to enlarge upon it from time to time.

Having completed your check list in privacy and having made your evaluation of your applicant, your next "persuasive aid" could well be a test of your own judgment. A probationary trial period is one way of doing this. You might test his self-control by placing him under pressure. By observation you can determine how your applicant responds to failure. By observation you can also determine how he reacts to success. Challenges often bring out the strengths and weaknesses of men. These can be "persuasive aids" for your evaluation. In fact, all measures you adopt to determine the selling ability of your applicant, or of members of your staff, are "persuasive aids" for making evaluations.

The ultimate test, however, of a man's ability to sell is whether he

*Traits revealed by*_____
*during interview with*_____*Date*_____

Positive Traits

_____FRANKNESS	Remarks:_____
_____NEATNESS	Remarks:_____
_____AMIABLE	Remarks:_____
_____OPTIMISTIC	Remarks:_____
_____COURTESY	Remarks:_____
_____PLEASANTNESS	Remarks:_____
_____HUMILITY	Remarks:_____
_____STEADINESS	Remarks:_____
_____GENTLENESS	Remarks:_____
_____SELF-CONTROL	Remarks:_____

Negative Traits

_____EVASIVENESS	Remarks:_____
_____UNKEMPT	Remarks:_____
_____ARROGANT	Remarks:_____
_____PESSIMISM	Remarks:_____
_____BRASHNESS	Remarks:_____
_____SURLINESS	Remarks:_____
_____BOASTFUL	Remarks:_____
_____ERRATIC	Remarks:_____
_____DOMINEERING	Remarks:_____
_____IMPATIENT	Remarks:_____

can go out and come back with the business in the bag. This is the point which is of primary concern to you as his sales manager and to him as a salesman. Sound evaluation is intended to uncover hidden talent which the sales manager can assist the salesman in developing to its fullest productivity.

An eminently successful insurance executive declared: "The first sales manager I worked for did me a great favor. He sold chemical products for institutional cleaning purposes. He worked me over thoroughly, tried me out, and then frankly told me I would never fit into his organization. He suggested that I investigate the insurance field. He thought I was adapted for that. Acting on his tip I discovered a place where I did fit in and to which I am now dedicated. I still consider that fellow who turned me away to be one of the greatest sales managers I have known. He was a persuasive guy. He built men. He also sold chemicals by the trainload."

Put Your Idea Across Persuasively by "Making It Come Alive"

Sales managers with records of breaking down barriers and building sales volume usually are masters of the art of persuasion. They vary in their methods of communication as they vary in individual personalities. Nevertheless, by following sound principles of communication they influence their sales people to achieve great things. They motivate them. They are dynamic, persuasive sales managers.

But, even among such successful sales managers there are those who have more difficulty than others in getting their ideas across to their staffs. One who struggled against such problems in communication came out of a sales meeting a disappointed man. He made this observation:

"What happened? I still believe my idea has merit. I tried to put it across. But it fell flat. Nobody got excited about it. Why?"

We did not hear this sales manager speak. We have no right to evaluate his effort. His problem appears to be a pretty common one among sales managers and other executives. A common expression among them is this: "If I could only put this idea across we'd have it made." The reason many good ideas fall flat or "wither on the vine," is that nobody makes them "come alive."

A case in point was Sales Manager "A". He was an impetuous man. He would call a meeting of his staff before his own idea had fully jelled in his mind. Result: A wandering, uninteresting, confusing, pointless presentation.

Another case in point was Sales Manager "B". He worked over an idea until it took complete possession of him. Then he would call his staff together. He would go into that meeting fired with enthusiasm. His business-promoting idea had become exciting to him. He drove home his points with the zeal of an evangelist. He cast out doubts. He hammered away on what his idea could do for his sales people. He showed them how to profit by it. He glorified the ultimate possibilities of his idea. He captured the interest of his listeners and he held on to that interest. He stimulated thinking. He aroused imagination. His whole idea "came alive." He paraded it before his sales staff in all of its alluring trappings. He caused them to *see* what a grand opportunity he had cooked up for them.

Here are the reasons *why* Sales Manager "B" put across his idea so persuasively:

1. *He touched the sensitive nerve of self-interest.* He impressed his staff by convincing them that his idea could become profitable for them. He dangled the lure of extra money before them. He stirred up their desire to have more. He

drew enticing mental pictures for them. He made it all very clear, very interesting, very attractive, very persuasive.

2. *He simplified his idea.* He screened out everything complicated which might blur the vision of his sales staff. He took no chances of being misunderstood. To accomplish clarity he made liberal use of graphs, pictures, sketches, and mechanical devices. He used anything which brought action into his presentation. He asked leading questions to test the understanding of his audience. He got his people involved in his discussion. He got them excited about his idea.

3. *He capitalized on action.* He used showmanship. He got movement into his "show." He submitted evidence to show that he knew what he was talking about. He was persuasive. He used visual aids and he made figures more meaningful so they would not "wither on the vine."

Sales Manager "B" spoke in a clear voice. When he drove home a point he thundered. When he moved nearer to his audience and became more persuasive he spoke softly, sincerely. He never mumbled. He kept his audience awake. He made his idea "come alive."

Until our own ideas excite us we risk becoming dull in our presentations. Case records in many fields provide evidence that worthy, well-developed ideas can be "sold" by making them appear to be significant, by making them "come alive."

Principle: Make your idea interesting, make it significant to your listeners, and make it believable. In this 3-pronged presentation you banish dullness, you make your idea "come alive."

Look to the "Balanced" Salesman for Persuasive Power

We are challenged to select men who can become highly productive in sales. This is the key to building a persuasive sales staff. To achieve this objective we become analytical. In effect we sit as judges. Then, having judged, we teach, direct, encourage, discipline and inspire men to *think big.* We motivate them to develop their persuasive power in order that they may persuade others to buy what they have to sell.

As a starting point we search for men who possess the following five elements upon which we can build successful careers in selling:

1. Good Health: Health habits are important in selling. Without health selling power is lost. With good health comes the drive and stamina to succeed.

2. Intelligence: This sublime quality, combined with good

health, reinforces the foundation on which we hope to build successful careers in selling.

3. Ambition: This is the driving force we look for in those who knock at our doors seeking to enter the fascinating realm of salesmanship. Ambition also gets sustenance from good health and intelligence.

4. Realism: This quality is the foe of wild notions about the "romantic life" of fictional salesmen.

5. Friendliness: This quality breaks down barriers which freeze out less congenial sales people. Friendliness is a marketable attribute. It is the art of handling people. It is the art of effectively exerting influence. It is the art of persuasion.

When sales managers find selling talent possessing the foregoing five qualities they reach out farther to uncover additional qualities such as these:

—*Industry*—It is decreed that salesmen, too, must work.

—*Integrity*—A durable, persuasive substance found in most successful salesmen.

—*Purpose*—The essence of motivation. It grows strong on a diet of goals, plans and zest for achievement.

—*Sincerity*—The persuasive spark which causes people to believe. It lights the way to sales volume.

—*Loyalty*—The salesman who is loyal to himself, to his family, to his sales manager, to his firm, to his product, and to his profession raises himself above mediocrity.

—*Imagination*—Of this dreams are made. Imaginative salesmen devise new and unique uses for whatever they sell. Perceptive sales managers encourage imaginative salesmen knowing that their dreams may have great potential in the market.

—*Ingenuity*—Sales barriers are challenges to ingenious salesmen. Eventually they find a way.

—*Initiative*—Self-starters have this quality in abundance. They're the "up and at 'em" type.

—*Patience*—The long-suffering salesman frequently bags the choicest pieces of business which some impatient salesman gave up as lost.

—*Balance*—In the foregoing qualifications for sales success we also have elements of the "balanced" salesman. Upon such "balance" sales managers develop highly productive selling teams, becoming dynamic sales managers through their capacity for developing in others the art of persuasion.

chapter 5

How to Stimulate a Flow of Market Tips by Persuasion

The sales manager of a commercial printing plant attributed his success to three factors:

1. Advance Market Tips.
2. Current, Relative Information.
3. Accurate Information.

"Our sources of information materially assist us in developing sales volume. Reliable advance tips of market developments open up areas for us whereby we can extend our service to prospective customers. Such tips often lead to definite sales commitments before competition gets on the job. Current information also serves as a check on our own competence. From such information we frequently find out how effectively we are functioning in our market. This is where accuracy is of importance. Inaccuracy may lead us astray, waste our time, waste energy, even lose sales. Accuracy is the basis of value of all market information."

Success in sales management leans heavily on information on which immediate action can be taken with profit possibilities. Such information may involve the obvious in the market. Or, it may involve situations such as these:

—Relationship of retailers to your operation.

—Relationship of distributors to your market and to your operation.

—Competitive activity in your territory.

—Attitude of consumers toward your products.

—Attitude of dealers toward your products.

—Attitude of your own salesmen toward your products.

—Attitude of your salesmen toward marketing problems identified with your territory.

Sales managers can profit by periodically giving serious consideration to this 3-point self-examination question: *How much do I really know about my market? Enough? Or, not enough?*

In developing a flow of market tips the following points become pertinent for effective sales management: (a) How much is your market yielding for you now? (b) How much is it capable of yielding? (c) How is your competition making out in your territory?

Adequate information about the economy of your territory enables you to act with wisdom and more decisively. You want to know whether the economy of the area you serve is steady, whether it is on the uptrend, or whether it is slipping. Such information should be available on call to sales managers. It must be current. It must be accurate. A steady flow of market tips provides an assurance of freshness.

There are methods of stimulating a flow of market tips. Such methods merit thoughtful executive attention because this matter involves profit possibilities.

One method of stimulating a flow of market information which has been productive for some sales managers might be called a "market intelligence system." Through such a system a flow of market tips can be stimulated by your own persuasive effort. By combining your individual efforts to obtain market information about your territory with the alertness and initiative of your field sales staff you have the makings of a productive "intelligence" system. You rely on your sales staff for sales volume. Why not for keeping you informed? They can become your "observation posts" in your territory. But, first they must be "sold" on the idea that a steady flow of market tips will benefit them materially, as it will benefit you and the house for which all of you work.

The objective of this system: To provide a workable method which can assure you, as sales manager, of a constant flow of "live" information about the territory from which you plan to develop increasingly profitable sales volume.

The action power available to you; as sales manager, to make this "sale" is the art of persuasion.

How to Build Market "Pipe Lines" by Persuasion

Productive market "pipe lines" are built by developing skills in observation and communication. This three-point objective is suggested for sales management in establishing and developing a free and adequate flow of market information:

1. To establish and maintain friendly relations with those with whom we deal. This includes customers, prospective customers, our sales teams, and, possibly, even our competitors.
2. To have and to encourage in others a reciprocal attitude. This includes our own administrative staffs as well as our sales teams. It also includes the administrative staffs of those to whom we sell or hope to sell.
3. To develop an alert, observant, analytical, and persuasively strong team of sales people.

Our first step in installing our market "pipe line" is to identify the probable sources of market information and then to develop those sources. Those who already buy from us rate the No. 1 spot on our list of such sources. The No. 2 spot is reserved for potential customers. In the No. 3 spot we can include competitors and others who have business ties with our customers and potential customers.

It is good business to maintain friendly relations with these sources of information. In time any of these sources may become highly responsive to our persuasive power and highly profitable. All of this spadework involves salesmanship—persuasive salesmanship. To reach the three-point objective we have set for ourselves becomes a major challenge for each individual on our selling team. Our confidence in them is a persuasive factor. We hire sales people, we train them, we direct them. We now propose to rely on them for a steady flow of market information.

The selling team is the key to building a productive market "pipe line." Sales managers have these field forces at their disposal. They can see them, hear them, evaluate them, and communicate with them. They can train them to observe and to evaluate. They can persuade them to communicate market tips which may prove to be profitable for the one transmitting such information and also for the others on the selling team.

If sales managers have been sufficiently persuasive to have "sold" this idea to their selling teams they have created the structure of a market "pipe line." Through this "pipe line" market information will flow to those sales managers. Field sales forces can stimulate a reciprocal attitude in those with whom they deal and thus widen their sources of information. This sort of unity is profitable and requires a high degree of persuasive selling to bring it into being, but it can be profitably productive for those who become so involved. The principle is simple: "We give in order that we may receive."

Reciprocity works something like this: We pick up the phone and give our friend down the line a tip which results in his landing a worthwhile piece of business. Our friend, feeling good will for us, reciprocates. He passes on to us a hot tip by which we similarly profit. Thus our "pipe line" is activated.

An alert sales team can uncover many sources of information which can enrich the sales manager's files and be used to benefit every member of his selling team. Among sources frequently overlooked by sales people are public records of mortgages, legal actions, real estate transfers, bankruptcies, bond elections, community actions, etc. If any of these affect in the slightest degree a customer, a potential customer, or a competitor, the sales manager should know about it. Newspapers, small and large, in communities in your sales territories can be rich in market tips. Persuade your sales people to read those publications.

To build market "pipe lines" and to keep them filled with information requires specialized training of sales teams. But this need not be complicated. By persuasion sales people can be made aware of the profit possibilities to them of being alert, of being observant, of being tactful. They can be trained in right and wrong methods of obtaining facts. They can be taught how to sift fact from rumor. They can be taught how to make out a simple report on their observations. They can be sold on the idea that this search for information is closely related to their searching for sales possibilities. The key to this selling job is the art of persuasion for sales managers.

The field of interest for observant salesmen is wide. Sales possibilities, market opportunities, distribution problems, transportation factors, development activity are all interrelated. Economic stability or instability, "boom" prospects or "bust" prospects are all of direct concern to sales managers, or should be. Even simmering discontent in an area is unwelcome information and yet an advanced tip of trouble may save trouble for those who sell.

Market tips of value are not restricted to favorable developments. Known in time, the unfavorable can often be turned to profit.

In profiting from market information flowing through your "pipe lines" the art of persuasion becomes your chief ally. For sales managers the art of persuasion has the power which can keep information flowing to them. And persuasive ability is something which can be developed.

With it good will can be established and maintained. Reciprocal relations can be strengthened by persuasion. The whole selling team becomes strong when it masters the art of persuasion.

Effective market "pipe lines," through which valuable market tips flow and benefit sales managers, salesmen, and the firms for which they work, are the by-products of the art of persuasion.

How to Convert Market Data into Sales by Persuasion

Let's get this straight: The motivation for rooting out market information is selfishness. Most of us have this trait. We want more sales. We want to get ahead faster. We want more pay, more profits. It's that simple. It's downright selfish, too.

If we can expose a given situation to the persuasive power of good salesmanship we, as sales managers, see additional profits sprouting in our fields which may have become barren.

We have learned from case records that adequate, reliable and timely market tips have served other sales managers well. We have an urge to get in on this bonanza. We have especially noted two ways in which the ready availability of reliable market data has been profitably productive:

1. By Stimulating Sales Growth.
2. By Establishing Safeguards Against Sales Losses.

One sales manager in the office supply business reports that information about a school expansion project enabled him to convert information into sales. "This involved a minor school improvement program," he said. "A reliable tip enabled us to get a head start on this matter. We got in on the ground floor and gave constructive assistance to the school authorities. What began as a small matter as the result of this tip turned out to be a respectable chunk of business. But the size of the initial order is not the important thing about this case. The significant point is that a market tip aroused us to opportunities which we had been ignoring. The relationship we established with this school board had far-reaching effects. Other school boards heard about the manner in which we served one board. This set up a chain reaction which created sales for us. It all resulted from exploiting a routine market tip."

A marketing specialist reports that he has seen sales possibilities uncovered by such bits of information as the following:

"As much as 30% of households in a given market area are without inside plumbing.

"Consumers here have buying power ranging all the way from semi-poverty existence to luxury-living standards.

"Restlessness is noticeable in some sections. People are heading out of the city to suburbia. Other people are leaving suburbia in increasing numbers, returning to the city.

"Home ownership here is high. Thirty miles from here it is low.

"Life insurance sales here are on the increase. In the suburban area life insurance sales have hit a new low.

"This is a stable market area. But, consumer incomes fluctuate seasonally from high to moderate."

The marketing specialist declares that each of these bits of marketing information suggests sales possibilities. Would similar market tips motivate your selling team to convert any of them into sales?

Perhaps you can convert more of the information now coming into your office into sales by more analytical, creative and persuasive selling. Perhaps with more vital information flowing through your market "pipe lines" you can develop even greater sales volume.

One method of using market tips to stimulate sales is to serve market data coming through your "pipe lines" to your salesmen in predigested form. For instance:

Salesman "A" has slipped. He passed up an opportunity by jumping at the conclusion that a bit of routine market data had no significance for him. It might have been possible for the sales manager to prod Salesman "A" into positive action by firing this question at him: "Have we got what it takes to get some business out of this deal?" This is a positive suggestion. Usually it has more persuasive power than a bawling out. It gently nudges the salesman to get with it. This is the art of persuasion for sales managers to get greater persuasive power out of their sales teams.

We convert market data into sales by a creative approach from all angles. A bit of information creates ideas. Those ideas stir up persuasive power. When skillfully applied, persuasive power results in sales. And, market data reaches the intensity of its value when it results in more sales.

Unfavorable developments are just as susceptible to profitable exploitation as favorable developments. Negative information challenges us to overcome this barrier to sales. Favorable information challenges us to make the most of the opportunity. In both instances persuasive power is the key to getting at the full riches of both positive and negative market tips.

Persuasive Devices for Gauging Market Coverage

A sales manager we knew became a community leader. He had established himself in his industry as a competent executive. He had surrounded himself with a sales team with productive capacity. Regardless of this progress this sales manager still was a dissatisfied man. He told his superiors why he was dissatisfied.

Sales had reached a plateau, moving neither up nor down. This irked this sales manager. His sales team appeared to have become smug, self-satisfied. This disturbed the sales manager. "I want more business," he told the board. "It's there to get. It will take some doing. But, I am convinced it can be done."

The board members nodded their heads, gave this sales manager a free hand, and he went into action to gauge his market and the coverage and the potential of his territory. He used many devices for giving him an accurate measurement. Here are ten of those devices:

1. Reports.
2. Surveys of His Market.
3. Experiences of Salesmen.
4. Research and Statistics.
5. Sales Forecasting.
6. Data and Estimates About New Products.
7. Analysis of Public Acceptance of His Own Products.
8. Analysis and Public Attitude Toward Company Policies.
9. Analysis of Production Records of Salesmen.
10. Competitive Standing in the Market.

From these ten sources this sales manager obtained a clearer picture of his situation. Some parts of that picture were deflating. This is often the case when anyone has basked too long under protective shelter. In such comfort one anticipates perpetual sunshine. He sees no clouds on the horizon.

Being a realist this sales manager accepted the challenge in what he had discovered to be the actual situation. To gauge how well or how badly he had been covering his market he set up three objectives:

1. To obtain, from sound research, the potential of his market for profitably using or consuming the products he sold.
2. To measure the total sales of his and all competing products in his territory.
3. To obtain factual data on how large a slice of his territory's business was going to his competition.

Would this sales manager now be satisfied with what was left after his competition had taken its slice of the business?

He had already given his answer to this question. He was not now, nor would he be satisfied with token success in the territory. He looked at the total potential of his market. That was the figure he was aiming at.

Realist that he was, he understood that he might fall short of total coverage of his market. But he could at least strive for that goal.

In searching for answers to his problem this sales manager turned to reliable research reports of which many were available. He obtained government reports on products which he sold. He dug into individual experiences of his salesmen. He made personal on-the-spot estimates of the various segments of his territory.

Having obtained adequate facts he sought out forecasts from those who had established reputations for accuracy. By correspondence and by personal visitations he obtained further measurements of how well he and his firm and his sales staff had served the territory. This data came from distributors, merchants, and direct from representative consumers.

These were the persuasive devices used by this sales manager. They shed light on the strong points and the weaknesses in this executive's sales organization, and in his policies and methods. Results were just as illuminating. These results included:

On Sales Coverage: That he had enough manpower.

On Effectiveness of Sales Coverage: That he fell short of satisfactory coverage. That he had a surplus of order-takers and a shortage of persuasive salesmen.

On Sales Training: That he had been deficient. That the mechanics of selling—report-making, order-writing, etc.—had been given precedence over developing persuasive skill in salesmen.

On Sales Direction: That there were executive weaknesses. That he had been unimaginative and uncreative in leadership. That he had failed to discern, to point out, and to define potential sales possibilities and to motivate his selling team.

On Self-Evaluation: That his executive weaknesses and weaknesses in his selling team could be charged up to an "all is well" attitude. That this could well be the product of too much comfort. That business had been good. That neither he nor his staff had been stirred up to go after greater and more profitable sales volume. That, being a realist, these deficiencies were the burden of sales management.

Result: This inquisitive and aroused sales manager, influenced by the persuasive devices he used to gauge his market coverage, changed his method of operation.

Objective: To go after more profitable sales volume instead of concentrating entirely on volume alone. Through the persuasive devices he employed to gauge his market coverage he became convinced that in many instances his sales volume appeared to be satisfactory but it was not altogether profitable volume. By exercising persuasive influence upon his entire selling team this sound objective was attained by this sales manager.

Research, charts, conferences, surveys, statistics, forecasts and a total awareness of new products coming on the market are tools for effective sales management. Each of these devices has certain persuasive power. The end result sought by dynamic sales management is *profitable sales volume.* This can be attained and is being attained through the selling power in the art of persuasion—a dynamic force for dynamic sales management.

Why Persuasive On-the-Spot Surveys Yield Higher Rewards

In the jargon of commerce few words are as loosely used as "survey." A sales manager is absent from his desk for a day or two. His expense account provides the answer. He was out on a "market survey." An advertising director catches a late plane and returns two days later. He was out on "a survey."

We are interested here in surveys that relate to sales. We discover, however, that many surveys are social engagements. These also have persuasive value in public relations. But, hard-knuckled market surveys are quite different. On-the-spot surveys are searching, penetrating inquiries and examinations. Their objective: To develop more profitable sales in a given area.

The hard-knuckled market survey is comprehensive and is based on this *who, what, how* survey plan:

1. Determine specifically *what* I want to find out.
2. Determine specifically *who knows most* about *what* I want to find out and *how* I can get through to him.
3. Determine *how* I can influence this person to yield *what* he knows about the market in which I am interested.

Communication is the key to success in any market survey. We must get through to those who have vital information which we require to advance our sales-building programs. Letters and telephone calls have been used effectively to reach distributors, dealers and selected consumers. But for a productive survey we need to do more than contact people. We must influence them by persuasive salesmanship. For this reason on-the-spot surveys have much in their favor. They yield such rewards as these:

1. *Direct Results.* They create confidence. The warmth in a handshake, in a smile, in a pleasant voice are persuasive, influential factors.
2. *Deep Insight.* On-the-spot surveys explore the built-in workings of the market—its character, its prospects, its problems.

3. *Exposure of Perils.* An on-the-spot survey quickly detects simmering disaffection in the market. The sales manager on the spot has the advantage of taking remedial action at once.

4. *Profitable Recognition.* Those interviewed in an on-the-spot survey are often flattered by being singled out for this purpose. They feel that they have been recognized for their importance. They may tell their friends, and this has persuasive sales value.

In this computerized age we still recognize the effectiveness of face-to-face communication. Were this not true we would have little excuse for sending forth salesmen to personally contact prospective buyers in our territories. The on-the-spot survey requires face-to-face contact in a *who, what, how survey plan.* It is the persuasive way. It yields high rewards.

Three Vital Plus and Minus Factors in Persuasive Management

A constant flow of meaningful market information assures sales management of an adequate supply of the substance from which profitable sales volume is developed. This constant flow results from training, persuasive stimulation, and persuasive motivation of sales personnel. Recognizing the value of such information let us also recognize three minus factors in sales management. But, first, let us consider these *plus* factors. They hold the keys to productive sales management:

1. *Selective Recruiting of Salesmen.* By surrounding yourself with imaginative, intelligent, personable personnel you lay the foundation for productive selling with a unified sales team alert to developments within your sales territory.

2. *Intensified Product Study and Sales Training.* Product knowledge, market requirements, market potentials, and an insight into the character of your territory are plus factors in sales management.

3. *Continuous Flow of Market Data.* Information (including market tips) are seen and understood by alert, observant, inquisitive, imaginative, creative salesmen. This is your "market intelligence team." If you have motivated them well to keep you informed of market developments you have another *plus* factor in your favor.

Now let us give stern recognition to the following trio of *minus* factors:

1. *Indifference* to market potentials and to individual sales

performance. Indifference at the management level in time contaminates the selling team with negative attitudes. Indifference to the value of market tips, to the persuasive value of merited praise for outstanding service, to the unity of the selling team is a destructive force.

2. *Communication Breakdowns.* Should your market information "pipe line" get clogged up it's a red light signal to get rolling with corrective action. It is also a green light for creative, inspiring sales management.

3. *The "All Is Well" Syndrome.* "When my salesmen get too comfortable I get uneasy," a sales manager in the electronics industry said. "When salesmen have no problems, no gripes, and drift into an 'all-is-well' attitude I fear that they are going to sleep. Success in my job is based on solving problems and training salesmen so they enjoy solving problems which I create for them to make them more productive, and eventually richer."

It's the *plus* factors in sales management that will produce adequate and reliable market information from the field and which will yield more profitable sales volume.

chapter 6

How to Exploit
New Territory
by Persuasion

A new sales manager had taken over. The subject of coffee-shop chit-chat was: "What sort of ideas will he be springing on us for getting business out of that new territory we're opening up?" Salesmen were anxious for an infusion of ideas from which they might benefit. They were anxious to exploit the new territory.

At his first conference after taking over, the new sales manager talked about finding new uses for the products of the house. Each of the new-use points he discussed he called "additions to the new territory."

He tried to get acreage out of the minds of his sales staff. They were prone to think about "new territory" solely on how many square miles they had to cover. "You are not shackled by boundary lines. Your territory includes the whole sphere of new uses from which our prospective customers can profit by more wisely using our products. Within the area which we propose to cover this is the unlimited expanse of our new territory—wider use of our products. We should never be oversold in that sort of territory.

"In my language," he explained, "exploiting new territory includes expanding the uses of our products. Of course we'll go into areas where neither you nor your competitors have thought of going before. We'll see the same people, but we'll sell them on new uses, new ideas for them to profit by. We'll find new areas of use for our products. This automatically gives us new territory. This offers us greater opportunities for increasing sales volume. We can attain these objectives by getting dry acres out of our minds when we speak about territory. Instead let us get the picture of expanding existing areas by making existing acreage yield more sales, profitably. Let us think about developing that new area, composed of new ideas for more uses of our products, to its full productivity for profit."

The formula for "exploiting new territory by persuasion" is a simple three-point recipe for building sales volume. The simplicity of this formula makes it persuasive. It adds no extra acres to what we call "our territory." It just adds more creative sales ideas.

Creative selling is inventive selling. Through it new uses for products are brought into being. These new uses become new areas for exploitation. With these new areas of uses new territory has been created without adding more acres. Here, then, is a simple three-point formula which can be used to exploit "new territory" by persuasion:

1. *Find New Uses.* Dig, innovate, invent, devise, observe, analyze. Do all manner of things to expand uses of what you have to sell. Get this message across to the whole selling team. Thus old territory will become new territory, and will become ripe for exploitation.

2. *Demonstrate.* With a flourish demonstrate to your selling team *how* your idea of beneficial usefulness opens up a whole new field for creative selling for them. Then, with similar flourish and with added enthusiasm send them forth to exploit this "new territory" which now includes acres, people and ideas. Pump life into the *newness* which you are now out to sell by convincing, persuasive demonstration to the sales team of how it can be done.

3. *Season with Persuasion.* Breathe into your demonstration the spectacle of showmanship. Give your demonstration and your whole presentation the sort of flash which will capture the attention of salesmen and start the machinery of creative thinking. When your salesmen have similarly aroused this "new territory" of new uses, generated interest in your ideas, and closed sales by persuasion, they have opened new areas to be further exploited.

Sales management's part in exploiting new territory consists of executive planning, of motivational direction, of creative thinking, of realistic communication.

Importance of "Bigness" in Persuasive Selling

"Bigness with the bulk of mankind is the nearest synonym for greatness," said Julius C. Hare.

Surely Mr. Hare was not intending to intimate that the poseur, the "big shot," is a symbol of greatness. On the contrary, no doubt Mr. Hare was attempting to elevate *bigness* to an impressive status.

Bigness is, in itself, impressive. It has a certain persuasive quality of its own. Bigness connotes strength and importance. This strength gives bigness persuasive force in selling. For instance, when we speak of the "big country" we create a picture of vast expanses of territory. When we speak of "the big company" our listeners visualize a commercial structure of size and strength. If we call a man "big" we can do so in a way which implies greatness, character and integrity. In this sense the "big man" label implies influence and takes on persuasive strength.

For sales managers "bigness" has persuasive power in a variety of areas, such as the following.

Big Salesmen

They are men who can tackle complex assignments and come back with the business all wrapped up. Big salesmen possess a certain quality of influence. This comes through persuasive power. Probably such salesmen perfected their persuasive power under the tutelage of big, persuasive sales managers. Because of this sort of bigness such sales managers frequently are referred to by their salesmen as "Mr. Big." In nowise is a sales manager so labeled because he poses as a big shot. Usually, should he be called "Mr. Big," it denotes that he has displayed qualities of greatness and his staff has profited by his greatness.

Big Sales Managers

"Great minds have purposes, others have wishes," wrote Washington Irving.

In the sales management field "Mr. Big" has a purpose.

We can hardly classify Admiral William F. Halsey as a sales manager, yet, in a sense, he did a lot of effective "selling." Those who served under Halsey testify that he had persuasive power. He was big in leadership qualities, which, of course, is what sales managers who are successful in their field also have—*bigness.*

"There are no great men," Admiral Halsey said, "only great challenges that ordinary men are forced by circumstances to meet."

Bigness in sales management is persuasive power which results in developing big salesmen.

A top management executive in the communications field said this about his executive sales director:

"There is what you can call a big man. There is nothing petty about him. We call him 'great' because he thinks big; he has big goals set up for himself and for his men. He develops little accounts into big accounts. He is big in human qualities. If one of his men suffers misfortune he shares in that man's pain. If one of his men hits the jackpot and comes in wearing a victory smile our sales director becomes more gleeful than the salesman. He goes wild over the victories of his men. He's just great!"

Bigness as a Selling Point

Yes, the bigness of the concern which you represent as its sales manager definitely is a selling point. You can safely tell your men to bear down on that selling point. You can tell them to build on that bigness. Explain to them and show them how to capitalize on bigness. The bigness of a house implies importance and strength. Selling points for exploiting this bigness include the following:

(a) Bigness can assure the buyer that there is strength behind the products you sell.

(b) Bigness can assure the buyer that there is integrity behind the products. Such bigness also implies that integrity had something to do with making it big.

(c) Bigness can give assurance to buyers that salable products will be available to meet market demands. The very bigness of a concern destroys any fear in a buyer's mind of dealing with a "fly-by-night" concern. This sort of bigness reflects stability. This carries persuasive power, an assurance of uninterrupted profit possibilities because bigness assures the buyer of adequate stocks on which to draw.

(d) Bigness assures mass promotion of products on a scale far greater, far more persuasive and far more effective than anything less than bigness could produce. Mass persuasion through advertising of the big company creates mass demand for its products. This shows up in dealer sales volume. Big sales managers capitalize on this factor in bigness. They sell the big idea to their selling team. They show their salesmen how to sell bigness to their accounts.

As a sales manager you and your staff can capitalize on bigness by making it important. You, and your selling team, can make bigness persuasive. As Mr. Hare wrote: "Bigness ... is a near synonym for greatness."

Tapping Reservoirs of Experience for Tested Methods

Exploitation of new sales territory requires understanding of attitudes, peculiarities, needs, wants, requirements and even intentions of buyers, distributors, and consumers of products and services. It requires knowledge of methods by which such territory may be made productive in sales. Many answers to questions arising in tested methods of achieving this desired result are found in reservoirs of experience. Sales managers in various fields profit by tapping those reservoirs.

In tapping reservoirs of experience sales managers have been known to show humility in the undertaking. Many who have witnessed this display of humility identify it with greatness. At any rate humility is often persuasive for it kicks out arrogance and quietly goes about the task of getting the job done.

Simply by the quiet, persuasive way of asking we may learn about new places, new things, new uses, new methods, new people, and about what makes people tick. In tapping reservoirs of experience by this persuasive method sales managers may find out how to reach and influence people and how to profitably increase sales volume.

A young man who was born to wealth was placed under the hammer by his father. He was required to go to work. The father's objective: To make his son self-reliant. He placed his son under a hard-nosed department manager in his factory. The department manager swamped the young man with problems. The young man, admitting his lack of specialized knowledge, sought help. He went to those who knew how to solve the problems that were pouring in to him. He tapped reservoirs of experience in the factory. He received guidance and he turned out to be eminently successful in his position.

As a sales manager you might ask: "What reservoirs of experience are available to me that I might tap?" As suggestions here are ten areas which you might explore:

1. *Urban Experience* for in-depth enlightenment about specified urban markets and how best to exploit them.
2. *Rural Experience* for information about consumer needs in specified rural areas and for data on distribution problems and sales problems which have been encountered by others in this market.
3. *Industrial Experience* for possible new approaches to more effectively penetrate this expanding market.
4. *Technical Experience* for enlightenment on tested methods of selling in this highly specialized field.

5. *Scientific Experience* for in-depth data on the possibilities of increasing sales in this market area.

6. *Mechanical Experience* for know-how on matters which may be alien to a sales manager's experience and training.

7. *Educational Experience* for guidance in setting up or improving sales-training methods. Also for new ideas on development of sales volume in the educational market.

8. *Administrative Experience* for guidance in streamlining office procedure and report-making requirements placed upon salesmen to the end that time might be saved for selling. Also for data regarding communication methods in this field.

9. *Fiscal Experience* for tested methods of economy in operation and for over-all fiscal efficiency in sales management.

10. *Legal Experience* for guidance in prevention of legal entanglements rather than getting you out of them. For counseling in legal problems arising out of exploring new sales territories and plans for exploiting those areas.

The methods of tapping reservoirs of experience are related to methods of stimulating a flow of market tips. (The building of market pipe lines was discussed in a previous chapter.) Both involve communication.

Contacts beyond as well as within your sales territory represent reservoirs of experience. Combined they form a vast reservoir which can be tapped by you with profit. On-the-spot surveys (also previously discussed) provide guidelines for tapping these reservoirs of experience. Such surveys often reveal the strength and the weakness in lines of communication.

A shrewd sales manager in the electric power industry once said: "It is a soothing sensation to know that I have knowledgeable, experienced friends strategically situated throughout my territory. They are involved in many lines of business. They have had vast experience in developing the areas we serve. It is satisfying to know that this rich source of information is available to me and is as near to me as my telephone."

Tapping reservoirs of experience for tested methods requires communication of a high order. By constantly extending our communication lines we insure for ourselves continuing access to reservoirs of experience. The actual method of tapping reservoirs of experience is relatively simple. We tap these reservoirs by asking. We present an opportunity to someone to share his knowledge with us. This compliment is persuasive and he shares what he knows with us.

For you in the sales management field this tapping of reservoirs of experience has rich possibilities for you. Not only can it extend your lines of communication but it can expand your possibilities for increasing profitable sales volume.

Essentially tapping of reservoirs of information is but one of many ways in which sales managers activate persuasive power. Through this persuasive power in action sales managers perform dynamically.

Tapping Inexperience for Fresh, Imaginative Ideas

"I'm going to crash that new territory with our top lines," vowed the sales manager of a furniture factory. "I intend to send inexperienced salesmen in there. I have an idea that their fresh ideas may pay off for me. It will be interesting to see how they make out."

This sales manager believed in challenges. This time he was tapping inexperience with a challenge. He had given those young, inexperienced men thorough theoretical training but they had experienced little sales-man-against-buyer contact. This sales manager had reason to suspect that those inexperienced young men had suppressed many of their ideas about selling in order to get along with veterans in the business with whom they had been associated during their training period. He sent those youngsters into the field recognizing that he was risking his own reputation on their performance.

Those youngsters went into the field. They did sell furniture in quantity. They were well received by dealers in the area they covered. They had literally crashed that new territory. As their sales manager in jubilation remarked: "Nobody had told them that they couldn't sell furniture out there."

Result: A new territory was opened up for their product. New accounts were established. These young men made good. They also made money. Their firm also cashed in on their inexperience.

How were they motivated to come through with such performance? By a challenge. The sales manager dared to send them out. They dared to tackle the unknown. It became an adventure. And, then, they had been given freedom to *think* their way through their problems.

Why they succeeded: They were possessed with youthful enthusiasm. Any risks they recognized only served to feed their enthusiasm. Opportunity to prove their own merit fed their enthusiasm. Opportunity to upgrade their standing as salesmen fed their enthusiasm. The lure of making money fed their enthusiasm.

Examining the case record of this venture in tapping inexperience we learn that three points contributed to its success:

1. *The Sales Manager had Vision.* He chose inexperienced men for a specific reason. He had confidence that they could think their way through a situation with a minimum of supervision. He believed that their fresh ideas, backed up by horse sense and enthusiastic work would carry them through successfully. He believed they would be responsive to a challenge.

2. *The Sales Manager had Persuasive Strength.* It was he who generated the spirit of accomplishment in those young men. He convinced them that he had opened a gate to opportunity. They took it from there.

3. *The Sales Manager Dared to Delegate Responsibility.* He delegated to young, inexperienced men important and specific responsibilities. This appealed to their pride. It was a stroke of far-seeing leadership. It was persuasive. It yielded high, cumulative returns from which the sales manager, the salesmen and the firm they represented all benefited.

The sales manager of a large western woolen mill sent inexperienced men into the back woods country. In logging camps, mining camps and in other remote settlements they sold blankets, overcoats, suits, dresses and knit goods. The idea came from the creative mind of the sales manager. Those remote spots had long challenged him. He had been aware that those people came to town to supply their *needs.* But he saw greater sales volume in satisfying their *wants* and *desires* rather than their needs. So he proposed to have inexperienced men carry samples of those products into the homes in those remote areas. They were friendly young men. They shook hands with these down-to-earth people. They made friends and they sold woolen goods. They created new wants and they built up desire for new things which they had to sell. They did all this in the friendly, informal atmosphere of those backwoods homes, in cabins, in trailers, even in tents and boarding shacks. Their performance confirmed that their sales manager had a live idea, that his confidence had not been misplaced, when he decided to take the risk of tapping their inexperience.

Certain risks are involved in tapping reservoirs of inexperience. It is understandable that sales managers may be reluctant to assume the risks of exposing sensitive territories to inexperienced men. It is not unusual that inexperienced men are timid about tackling the unusual. Some of them worry about what others may think of them if they break away from routine and attempt a new angle in selling.

One sales manager explained the problem this way: "Sure I took a chance. Of course I was jittery. But it was worth it. How else could I have found out so much about my territory and the capabilities of my men?"

This sales manager's remark echoes what Thomas A. Edison once said: "I know several thousand things that won't work." Edison is also said to have failed 10,000 times before he made the incandescent light work.

Principle: Persuasive selling power may lie dormant in inexperienced men. This reservoir of inexperience can be tapped by a challenge and by persuasion.

Testing Sales Ideas for Persuasive Power

From whatever source you get a sales idea you probably will ask this question about it: "Will this sell?"

That's a reasonable question. Let us find out whether your last idea, seemingly born out of nowhere, had any persuasive sales value. We can do this by testing.

Testing is an IFY business, so here are ten IF'S for testing your sales idea. They will illuminate the persuasive power of an idea. They will assist you in maintaining a practical, creative approach to determining what persuasive power your sales idea may have. For, if it lacks persuasive power it lacks a necessary ingredient to make it sell. Put your idea through these ten IFY steps to test its sales power:

1. IF it supplies a need it is persuasive.
2. IF it satisfies a want it is persuasive.
3. IF it promises beauty, good taste, strength, safety, harmony, fun, or adventure it is persuasive.
4. IF it promises material rewards it is persuasive.
5. IF it promises happiness or better health it is persuasive.
6. IF it arouses ambition, or stirs up action it is persuasive.
7. IF it promises personal security or progress it is persuasive.
8. IF it suggests better ways of doing business it is persuasive.
9. IF it promises prestige, comfort, status, increased income, or other contributions to personal well-being it is persuasive.
10. IF your sales idea is a positive one and IF it promises benefits in any way to those who buy or use whatever you have for sale it is persuasive.

The ideal selling staff is one that is rich in persuasive ideas for selling. The source of these ideas matters little. You may get most of your ideas out of the idea suggestion box. Your competitor may have ideas flowing in to him from his salesmen in the field. If so it is apparent that he has built his idea pipe line well. He has established . productive lines of communication. It is possible that your most productive sales ideas have come to you through the process of association. You may have witnessed some sales technique at work in a field other than your own. This interested you. You related this technique to your own lines. As a result you came up with a fresh approach to selling your products or services. This is why we hear so much about *creative thinking* in selling.

Creative thinking is the sales manager's greatest challenge. It is the enemy of peddling. It turns thumbs down on order-taking as a substitute for persuasive selling. It removes dullness from selling.

The persuasive power in any sales idea is how well it appears to make life more stimulating, more rewarding, more productive for those who buy or use what you have to sell. By discovering how the buyer can be benefited you discover a new source of wealth for yourself. This is when persuasive power has its greatest hour. Test your sales ideas to determine IF they have this sort of persuasive power.

An additional contribution to testing sales ideas is this simple formula:

   —Subject your idea to a How Test. *How* will your idea yield benefits to those to whom you propose to sell it?
   —Subject your idea to the ten-point IFY Test previously outlined for determining the persuasive strength in a sales idea.
   —Subject your idea to the Why Test. Refine your sales idea. Bring it down to earth. Simplify it. Get your staff stirred up about your idea in a positive way. Test it and re-test it for persuasive power. With that it will sell!

Hidden Profits in Acres, People, Persuasion and Sales

Sales managers, challenged by the possibilities for profit in new sales territories, have four additional challenges. Let us examine them:

1. The challenge of acres.
2. The challenge of people.
3. The challenge of opportunities for increasing sales volume.
4. The challenge of mastering the art of persuasion.

A sales manager's territory can be loosely defined as the boundaries of the area which has been assigned to him for exploitation and development into a profit-producing market.

Within the boundaries of those acres which challenge him are people. These people constitute the sales manager's No. 2 challenge, if not his first. These people hold the power of success or failure for any sales effort which may be aimed at those challenging acres.

The sales manager's objective is, or should be, to utilize those acres for profitable ends. In other words, he is out to exploit those acres until they become high-yield territory for him and his selling team.

The sales manager of a brand-name bedding manufacturing firm revealed the secret of his success at a sales conference he had called. He said that the spectacular sales-production record of his whole selling team was due to just three factors:

1. The lure of searching for hidden profits.
2. The people who hold the solution to the riddle of hidden profits.
3. Closing of sales—the ultimate goal, the ultimate victory of those who engage in exploiting and developing new sales territory.

This successful sales executive elaborated on his triple-factor success secret in this way:

"To get at hidden profits in our territory we have had people and motives going for us. We have a tightly knit sales team, excellent communication, and a lot of ginger to keep us driving toward our objectives.

"Our highest yields on acres which we call our territory are from what we refer to as 'hidden profits.' These sales came from those previously undeveloped spots which had been overlooked by us and others. Hidden profit territory is wide open for sales exploitation. By utilizing for profit what had otherwise been nonproductive areas we have created a responsive market for our product.

"At the bottom of all this effort is dynamic, persuasive selling. This I have found must be motivated by the sales manager. To get top production out of salesmen we need to keep them well fed with sales ideas that excite them. We do this by demonstrating to them how to present profitable ideas to dealers and to potential dealers. We show them how they can demonstrate productive sales methods to their sales staffs. All of this adds up to persuasive selling.

"When you have acres with potentials, people with potentials, plus the temptation to pile up sales records with a liberal dose of persuasive sales power, we believe you can sell the idea of more restful sleep, the idea of sleeping comfort, the idea of a mattress contributing to better health. Yes, and you can sell anything else by the same technique of persuasiveness."

chapter 7

How to Motivate
Salesmen to
"Reach for the Sky"
in Selling

Knute Rockne, famed football player and coach, once declared that fear of competition is a big problem in business as well as in sports.

If we accept Rockne's viewpoint we may turn his statement to profitable account in sales management. If fear of competition obstructs our path to success then we must get rid of fear. This means that the destructive force of fear must be erased from the minds of men whom sales managers direct. This presents a formidable challenge in persuasion to sales management.

When a man is seated in a sales manager's chair he becomes a teacher. Can he measure up to that challenge? His selling team expects inspiration from him. Salesmen expect him to provide them with new goals. They want him to reveal the secrets of success to them. They want to know how to sell more.

This, then, becomes a continuing burden on sales managers. They are charged with motivating their selling teams to "reach for the sky" in selling. The following five points may assist sales managers who have picked up the challenge to motivate salesmen:

1. They can present to salesmen understandable and workable ideas. These ideas may include the rules, the ethics and the purposes in human relationships.
2. They can set up goals. In clear terms they can point the way to selling success with no guarantees.
3. They can chart the routes by which objectives may be reached with no guarantees that they will be reached.
4. They can expose obstacles which may be encountered along the way.
5. They can detail the resources which must be drawn on by salesmen to keep them moving ahead toward the goals which have been established.

The ghost of fear which Knute Rockne said was a problem in business now becomes a motivating factor for resourceful and imaginative sales managers. Persuasive power is often bottled up by such resistance as competition. That form of resistance can motivate men to overcome it. Faced with resistance the embattled salesman may cry out, "I'm going to crack that guy's record," or "I'm going to get business out of that prospect if it takes all winter." When this happens to a salesman he usually eggs himself on to success. His sales manager may be able to reinforce the salesman's fighting spirit.

What else can a sales manager do to motivate his selling team to greatness? Here are seven suggested ways for motivation:

1. *Necessity.* Stir up the "must do" spirit.
2. *Courage.* Crush fear. Only the courageous "reach for the sky" and attain their goal.
3. *Timidity.* Even a shy salesman can be persuasive. However, timidity often lacks the driving power necessary for success in selling. The timid salesman presents a major challenge to sales management. The sales manager may have the necessary skill to bring out other qualities in the timid soul which have persuasive power which can be converted into sales.
4. *Conviction.* Here's where the persuasive strength of the sales manager shows up. The selling team must *believe* if it is to *sell.*
5. *Sense of responsibility.* Here is something for sales management to nourish in all salesmen.
6. *Optimism.* Another quality requiring periodic nourishment.

Helen Keller, the humanitarian, once said: "Optimism is the faith that leads to achievement."

7. *Purpose.* A clearly defined purpose is loaded with motivating power. Make it worthwhile to salesmen. Make it tough to attain, but attainable. Encourage salesmen to "reach for the sky."

In all of this we discern why sales management requires teaching of a high order. Through inspirational teaching and direction, sales teams can be aroused to "reach for the sky" in selling.

Teaching, however, requires more than facts. Teaching requires more than knowledge. Effective teaching requires spirit—the spirit which inspires men to "reach for the sky." When salesmen are inspired to look upward, when they are inspired to tackle the seemingly impossible, they will eventually arrive at the high goal.

Inspired leadership can alter negative viewpoints. Salesmen can be persuaded to become optimists. They can be convinced of the profit possibilities in working harder. Inspired leadership can give them sustaining courage when the day has gone against them. The doubtful can be made to believe in what they are selling. They can be made to believe in their own ability to sell it. Inspired leadership can replace timidity with determination. Constructive motivation can give men a sense of responsibility which provides them with fuel for self-motivation.

With purpose in their work, with this purpose made clear and persuasive to them, salesmen can be motivated to "reach for the sky." Moreover, they can attain high goals. Because they were given a purpose, because they were shown the way and because they had become convinced that rewards were great and were attainable for them, they set their sights high and "reached for the sky."

In this way dynamic sales managers are made. They are cast in the roles of persuasive teachers and dispensers of motivation for salesmen. They play their parts well and they find their reward in expanding sales volume and also in the achievements of others on their selling teams.

Sales Power of the Skillful Tempter

Sales managers in virtually every area of business have exerted pressure in some form to motivate salesmen. In this area persuasion has been productive. Persuasive power often casts the persuader in the role of a tempter. For example: The tempter tries to induce a salesman to sell more. Among sales managers the skillful tempter accomplishes his purpose in six steps:

1. He begins by setting up a sales target.
2. He assigns target areas to chosen salesmen.
3. To those chosen salesmen he specifies all known sales possibilities which he intends to exploit in those target areas.
4. He outlines to his chosen selling team an overall sales strategy for his operation. He also suggests persuasive selling techniques.
5. He throws down a challenge to his chosen sales team.
6. He appeals to the self-interest of his selling team. He frankly and honestly tells them what is in it for them. He bids for full scale exploitation of all areas of his sales target by announcing incentive rewards for outstanding sales performance.

As you see temptation is involved in each of the foregoing six steps. The target itself is tempting to the sales team.

A sales manager in the lumber industry once said: "A definite sales goal is always an incentive for salesmen. Nobody really enjoys sitting on the sidewalk watching a victory parade. They want to be part of it. It's that way in selling. I set up an attractive target spotted with challenging difficulties, and then I turn to my salesmen and say: 'Go get 'em.' If I have made the target tempting enough they'll come back with business."

By assigning target areas to chosen salesmen you establish a competitive spirit without saying so. Each salesman wants to make a favorable showing. It motivates them to "reach for the sky."

You show skill in tempting by specifying sales possibilities. You invite each salesman to get his share of the pie to be cut.

You further reveal skill in tempting by disclosing your overall sales strategy. Each man on the team worth his salt will be striving to be a top producer.

Nothing is more persuasive than a challenge to win rich rewards by personal effort. Pride is involved here. Self-interest, also. Tempting? Of course it is.

The skillful tempter is a persuasive fellow. Case records show how sales managers profit by skillfully tempting their sales teams to "reach for the sky" in scoring sales records.

Your Dual Persuasion Problem: The Future and Today

Henry Ford once said: "Nobody can really guarantee the future."
Nevertheless most sales managers feel that they are expected to be able to make reasonably accurate forecasts of sales volume. This presents

what has been called a dual persuasion problem. The sales manager must persuade both himself and his superiors that he is on the right track in sales development.

The future with its secrets constitutes a problem for you as a sales manager.

Today is another problem, including what you are going to do about today.

Dale Carnegie suggested that we live in "day tight compartments" to overcome worry. Living a day at a time may have its virtues but sales managers would still be haunted by uncertainties.

One sales executive who had an enviable record in training and motivating salesmen said the dual persuasion problem was more complex than shutting out tomorrow and living just for today. "For example," he said, "I have one salesman who constantly worries about what he must face tomorrow. If I give him assignments for tomorrow his sales drop off today. He dissipates his energy by fretting over what may happen to him in the future.

"Then I have another man," this sales executive continued, "who thrives on future assignments. If I give him assignments for tomorrow, or for next week, he tears into his work for today. Moreover, he usually comes up with record sales for today. You see, he thinks in terms of getting all he can out of today as a means of clearing the way for a heavy schedule tomorrow. He is motivated by anticipation of a heavy future schedule to work harder today. He doesn't worry about tomorrow. He plans for it."

The future has a way of frightening some salesmen and this, in turn, becomes a sales management problem. John Glenn, Jr., the astronaut, shed some light on this. He maintained that people are afraid of the unknown. But, he added: "If a man faces up to it and takes the dare of the future he can have more control over his destiny." There is an element of encouragement in that statement for you as a sales manager when you are confronted by the dual persuasion of today and the future and what to do about it.

John Glenn, a "sky man" in his own right, made another observation which should motivate both salesmen and sales managers to "reach for the sky" in sales training, in sales direction, in self-motivation, and in solving dual persuasion problems. Glenn said that we might call today an age of curiosity, in which inquiry and imagination are leading to vital discoveries. Surely curiosity, inquiry and imagination in sales management and in salesmanship can contribute to the effectiveness of sales planning for today and also for the future.

Motivation of salesmen to "reach for the sky" is a challenging opportunity for every sales manager. It requires wisdom to deal with dual persuasion problems. These problems affect today's sales and future production as well. But the record shows that such problems can be solved. They are being solved by imaginative, far-seeing sales executives who have mastered the art of persuasion.

Principle: To motivate salesmen to "reach for the sky"—*know them well.*

Pick up the challenge yourself of tackling the dual persuasion problem. In the same way as sales objections are converted to selling points, your salesmen can banish doubts of the future. They can do this if you motivate them to prove that today can be a record-breaker in sales production. Then, convince them that tomorrow is a continuance of today.

Dead-End Streets Present Persuasive Challenges

When our plans wind up in a "dead-end street" our curiosity is aroused. Momentarily we feel that our dreams have been only bubbles and worse, that those bubbles have now burst. We wonder why. For us, as sales managers, this need not be the end of dreaming. We still are curious. The "dead-end street," which is holding us up, is just a temporary blockade.

Albert Einstein, the scientist, said: "The important thing is not to stop questioning. Curiosity has its own reason for existing." In this Einstein has given us an incentive to continue to motivate our sales teams.

One sales manager who directs a sales team in three states contacting virtually every sort of business enterprise which can profitably use promotional material ran into a "dead-end street." Said he: "This had happened to me before. I have learned that even 'dead-end streets' are populated by prospects. Any resourceful salesman will find them. He will also sell to them. Of course, my dream which got sidetracked in that 'dead-end street' turned out to be just a bursting bubble. However, even a bursting bubble can stimulate a dreamer. It can motivate him to give his idea another try."

Contests are favorite sales stimulators with many sales managers. A recent survey disclosed that contests arouse a measure of curiosity among participating salesmen. Even those contests which have been stalled in "dead-end streets" produced some benefits. The greatest benefits came from well-organized, well-conducted, and fully steamed up contests which aroused curiosity among participants.

When sales incentives arouse curiosity, and that curiosity is coupled with enthusiasm and with artful persuasion, they accomplish at least three worth-while things:

1. They motivate salesmen to act.
2. They increase sales. Whether sales increase is sustained is beside the point. The fact remains that the incentive device caused sales to go up.
3. They arouse curiosity. Participants wanted to know why the uptrend stopped. At that point we have a challenge to sales management. If any device which may be employed to stimulate sales increases sales then it must have had some sales value. It is worth exploring.

Let us assume you are now stalled on a "dead-end street." Your sales promotion dream has been as shattered as a bursting bubble. Experience comes to your rescue. You can retrieve it all by meeting this **A, B, C** challenge:

A. Find the element of sales merit which resulted in the temporary increase in sales. Lay it bare. Examine it closely.
B. Reevaluate your dream. Reexamine that element of sales value that you discovered. Eliminate its weaknesses. Find its strongest and most persuasive points.
C. Exploit that element to the ultimate degree. Motivate your sales team to pull your sales dream out of the "dead-end street." Subject the salable element which you have discovered to the full power of persuasive salesmanship.

The Motivating Power in Status Appeal

The sales manager of a concern which goes after business in most states in the union published a monthly "status sheet." The purpose of this publication was to motivate salesmen. It presented the relative standings of the top ten salesman, each month. Ratings were based on sales closed.

Salesmen in that concern and also in competing concerns saw the motivating power in that "status sheet." Here are some of their reactions:

—The "status sheet" motivated the top ten to write enough business to hold on to their ratings.
—Nine of the top ten were motivated to write enough business to reach the top spot of the top ten.
—Other salesmen in the organization were motivated to write enough business to rate a spot among the top ten.

—The "status sheet" established a persuasive objective. It motivated all salesmen to become success-minded. It tempted salesmen with the possibility of making more money. It presented case records showing how sales had been increased. It placed a premium on initiative and accomplishment.

The status appeal gets close to a man's desire to "be somebody." This isn't an indication of immaturity. All salesmen won't rate spots on a top ten "status sheet," but every salesman can aspire to greatness.

—*Fame* is involved in the status appeal.

—*Reputation* is involved in the status appeal.

—*Pride* is involved in the status appeal.

—*Success* is involved in the status appeal.

The status appeal challenges the best that is in a man to rise above mediocrity. It challenges a salesman to become a lead man, to be a winner, to be a producer.

Master salesmen have used the status appeal to sell such things as investment securities, life insurance, home-study courses, and many other products and services.

Sales managers with vision capitalize on the desire to rise above the herd. Through the art of persuasion they motivate salesmen to "reach for the sky," to rate a spot among the top ten. The status appeal is loaded with the sort of persuasive appeal which puts sales on the uptrend and keeps them there.

Motivating and Sales Power in Sales Contests

Sales contests can and do produce profitable results. Sales managers have built up sales volume on a sustaining basis by developing the competitive spirit to motivate salesmen.

As we have previously noted a few contests may wind up in "dead-end streets." This need not be fatal. It does not eliminate the sales contest from the sales production line.

Competition is the motivating power in contests. Competition whets a man's desire to prove that he can do it. It becomes a game with him. It's the "I'll show the world" spirit in action. He is out to excel. He craves attention (the status appeal). In competition he has a purpose. Sales contests are closely tied in with the status appeal.

The *selling power* in sales contests has been demonstrated. Sales contests are not new. We are chiefly concerned with the successful contests. Successful contests have motivating power. Behind the successful contest is the energy of persuasive power. And this presents to sales management one of its great challenges.

A salesman in the soft drink industry came to his sales manager with this observation: "This contest we are all wrapped up in is a real swinger. My customers are talking about it all over my territory. They want to know how I'm making out. They're talking about me, about the firm, and about our 'pop.' They're bringing new customers to the stores where our 'pop' is sold. These gabbing people are also tempting a lot of people to become 'pop' drinkers."

In many instances sales are stimulated by the same persuasive power which motivates salesmen to work harder at selling.

Automobile contests launched by some dealers with the introduction of a new model have motivated salesmen to "reach for the sky." The competitive pitch has aroused their enthusiasm. They talk to a prospective car buyer in such persuasive terms as these:

"*Be first* in your neighborhood to own this car. Think of the pride of your wife and your kids when you bring this car home. Right now we have a full choice of colors. With this sales contest going as it is we may not be able to deliver every color tomorrow."

"*For top trade-in on your car this contest is a money-maker for our customers.* You can get in on the ground floor of these special trade-in deals. We are making extra high trade-ins to introduce this new model. You probably have heard that we are in a 30-day introductory sales contest. This is it. The first showing of this new model. Full choice of colors. Low special terms. High special trade-ins during our sales contest. . . ."

"*By acting now you'll be the first* among your associates at the Country Club to show up in this new sports model. Isn't it a beauty? Today you have a choice of all five colors on this model. They'll go fast during our sales contest which we opened up with this morning."

Status appeal plus the sales contest idea provides a persuasive combination in situations such as the foregoing and also in the following case of selling to dealers:

"*Be among the first dealers* in this area to bring this new product to your territory. You're reading all about this product now in five great national magazines. Your customers are seeing it and hearing about it on TV. This is your opportunity to tie up with this product in this great selling campaign. To give still more selling kick to this product we are all excited about our 60-day sales contest to tie in with the national campaign to introduce this product. Let me go over these quantity-purchase advantages we have for dealers. . . ."

Sales contests can also have dual persuasive power:

1. *Contests can motivate salesmen* through the stimulating power of the competitive spirit.

2. *Contests stimulate selling* by capitalizing on the status appeal. But, this does not exhaust the persuasive power in sales contests. When sales teams become fully motivated to excel in a spirited contest you have generated—created—persuasive power for attaining new sales records.

Five Positive Ways for Self-Motivation

A young sales director in the insurance field discovered that self-motivation had cumulative persuasive power.

"Whenever I note a let-down in sales I take myself in hand. 'Look here,' I say to myself, 'what has happened to my leadership? How can I reverse this trend? How can I influence my salesmen to put more drive into our selling program?'

"This sort of self-scolding often jerks me up short. It opens my eyes. More important it has a tendency to change my attitude toward lagging salesmen. Instead of bawling them out I accept partial responsibility for their failures. I also find a challenge in those failures. So, I get down to brass tacks with those salesmen. I probe deeply to find out what has caused their let-down. I try to infect them with selling fever. When they catch this fever they go out, they make calls, and they sell."

Sales managers in most fields of commercial activity have their pet methods of self-motivation. Some capitalize on temporary defeat. Others get enthusiastic over a gain in business. The latter take a small gain as a challenge to do even better. Some are motivated by the progress of a salesman they have trained. Others are motivated to improve their training programs.

We have selected five suggestions for sales managers. These are motivation ideas which have been tested. One or more may not directly apply to you at this time, but they may later. Your leadership status and power is at stake here. Consider these suggestions for self-motivation:

1. Clearly define your objectives.
2. Become involved in the hopes, aspirations, problems and *capabilities* of each member of your sales team. Through sincere, personal interest in your salesmen you will learn more about their latent strength on which they and *you* can capitalize.
3. Reevaluate yourself often. Constantly evaluate your training methods, your management methods, your policies, and your over-all selling program. Expose the weak spots in both training and performance. Examine these. Expose the strong points and more fully exploit them.

4. Maintain total command of yourself, of your position, and of your selling team. Develop discernment. Seek out new possibilities for sales development, for stronger leadership, for more effective teaching to accentuate personal persuasive power.

5. Revise your objectives. Eliminate those which, from time to time, fail to excite you. Reinforce your objectives until your whole purpose becomes clearly established. Then dare yourself to put it across. This is the essence of self-motivation. It is also the basis of dynamic sales management.

How Persuasion Can Unshackle Self-Interest and Awaken Dynamic Sales Power

Sales managers who aspire to become dynamic in their executive field become goal-setters, problem-solvers, teachers, and motivators. Their success stems from their persuasive power in salesmanship and in leadership.

Encouragement, they find, has persuasive force. Sales managers with vision encourage initiative in salesmen who are striving for individual improvement. They encourage self-reliance, creativity, constructive imagination, loyalty.

Discouragement, they also find, has persuasive power. Sales managers with initiative and leadership qualities recognize discouragement as a personal challenge. This negative force can arouse one to banish fear and to crush indifference. We can discourage discouragement by recognizing the folly of self-satisfaction, the profitless folly of dullness, the barrenness of disinterest. At all cost, both sales manager and salesman need greatly to discourage within themselves the thought that "this is good enough."

Maximum persuasive power lies in a higher goal for tomorrow than the one you arrived at today.

Self-interest is the gateway to effective persuasion. In the words of one sales manager who reached the top in the aluminum industry: "When I finally found out that each salesman on my staff held part of my future in his ability to sell I began to make marked headway in sales management."

This sales manager was motivated by self-interest. "What's there in it for me?" becomes a vital question in sales management and in salesmanship. The answer to that question holds the key to persuasive power. When we learn how to appeal effectively to the self-interest of another we satisfy our own self-interest and become more persuasive.

By relating a salesman's opportunities to greater personal gain a sales manager unshackles that salesman's self-interest. Dominated by self-interest the salesman releases his persuasive power and both he and his sales manager stand to benefit.

An investigator for a management syndicate saw how shackled self-interest kept some men of talent from rising above mediocrity. He explained: "Nobody had ever taken the time to appeal strongly to the self-interest of those men. Once they were convinced through persuasion that they were capable of achieving more, and enjoying more of the world's goods than they were getting, they responded productively and both they and their sales managers mutually profited."

The general sales manager of a large department store in an ocean-side west coast city came into the women's shoe department at a moment of crises. One salesman was under fire from a hostile customer. The salesman's persuasive power was activated by the woman's unhappiness over a previous purchase. He soothed her. She went out smilingly satisfied. The salesman was pleased. So was the general sales manager. Another salesman was trying to please a fussy, discriminating prospective customer. This salesman had piled up seven pairs of shoes, all boxed. He had placed all of those shoes on that woman's feet at least once. Suddenly the woman got up and left without buying. The frustrated salesman was muttering to himself when the general sales manager approached him and asked: "How did you lose that sale?" The salesman snapped: "I wouldn't know. I pulled out every style we had in her size and the color she wanted. I tried them on, but she didn't go for any of them."

"What shoe did you try to sell to her?" the sales manager persisted.

"I told you. I tried on seven pairs. She just didn't buy. It's as simple as that."

"Not quite," the general sales manager said. "When did you complete our sales training course?"

"I have never taken it. Didn't know about it."

This motivated the sales manager to have this man assigned to a special training class. The sales manager's interest unshackled that man's self-interest. The special training he received awakened his inherent sales power. Self-interest motivated him to "reach for the sky." This same motivation carried him up to his self-established goal—a position in sales management.

In sales management the art of persuasion is a dynamic force for motivating salesmen to aspire to greatness. This is the constructive objective of sales management—to appeal to the self-interest of the selling team.

Sales managers become enthusiastic about motivating their sales teams because the whole idea of developing sales volume appeals persuasively to the sales managers.

Principle: Unshackle self-interest and you thereby activate persuasive power—the force which produces dynamic sales managers and high volume salesmen.

chapter 8

How to Criticize a
Salesman's Performance
with Constructive Persuasion

Criticism can be a persuasive force in perceptive and persuasive sales management. We find the fullness of this persuasive power neither by using it as a club nor by applying it as a soothing balm.

In sales management we have one objective: *Produce more sales.*

This applies to criticism, for if, by inept criticism we destroy initiative in a salesman, we injure that salesman and penalize ourselves. "It is much easier to be critical than to be correct," Benjamin Franklin warned us.

Criticism can be both constructive and persuasive. We can point out error without being abusive—simply by suggesting a better way. As Samuel Johnson defined it, "Criticism is a study by which men grow important and formidable at very small expense."

When we criticize the performance of a man who has confidence in his own ability as a salesman we must, in our own selfish interest, safeguard that man's self-confidence, for on that we can capitalize. If what he has done has hurt sales or has injured his stature as a representative of the firm, we have a teaching job to do. We also have this salesman's pride, his sensitive nature, his past performance and his capabilities to consider.

The advertising director of a large newspaper used diplomacy in handling delicate problems. "When an otherwise competent salesman muffs the ball what can I gain by blowing up?" he asked. "I could rile him so he'd stop selling for a day or two. What profit would there be in that? Would it pay me to tear into him for losing one inning in the ball game? He feels tough enough about the blunder because he's not the blundering type. In situations such as this, one big question pops into my mind: I ask myself how I can prevent repetition of such blunders. How can I show this man how he can avoid them? How can I show this man how to polish his sales technique and make it shine? How he can be more tactful? How he can become more persuasive? If I can get this line across to him I can cash in on his blunder. After all, I am selfish about this deal. I want him to get this error off his back. I want him to sell more advertising space. That's my objective in my job—to build salesmen, not to knock them down."

The very act which may cause one salesman to lose out with one prospective buyer may be successful with another. For this reason the art of being both constructive and persuasive in criticism presents a major challenge. It involves the following 11 areas and perhaps more:

1. *Persuasiveness.* Influence others to be more productive. Sell them on a better way.
2. *Tolerance.* Recognize the position and view of the man facing you across the desk. Respect his position and his views.
3. *Direction.* Show him how it could have been otherwise— how it could have been more profitable to him.
4. *Judgment.* Know and understand the man and his problems.
5. *Selfishness.* Bear in mind that your salesman's success means your success.
6. *Obedience.* Have rules of procedure, rules of conduct, policy rules, and, then, firmly and persuasively require compliance with those rules.
7. *Conformity.* Your sales team probably includes a man, or men, who are strict conformists. They follow the herd. They lack originality. Should you criticize them, or should you persuade them to develop initiative? Your leadership is at stake here.
8. *Non-conformity.* Was your errant salesman guilty of non-production or non-conformity? Wasn't it possible that he was exploring new areas for sales production? You ought to know.
9. *Plain Talk.* Speak and write in such a way that you will be understood beyond question. Be sure you are understood before you criticize.

10. *Humility.* Even a sales manager can profit by this virtue. It's priceless when criticism becomes necessary or desirable.
11. *Discernment.* See the problem clearly before you criticize. Try to see it from his point of view as well as yours. Discernment leads to constructive persuasiveness.

How to Make Criticism a Strong Ally

A sharp dividing line should separate criticism and faultfinding. Even in a critical mood the sales manager will profit more by striving to inspire salesmen. He will show them how they can do better than they have been doing. He will show them how they will materially benefit by such improvement. But faultfinding riles rather than inspires. It cools rather than warms the spirits of men. Faultfinding dampens enthusiasm. Constructive criticism sheds a warm glow on a man's weaknesses. He sees a way out. He isn't humiliated.

Charles Schwab, the great American industrialist, had some thoughts on criticism which apply to many problems of sales management. He said: "I have yet to find a man, however exalted his station, who did not do better work and put forth greater effort under a spirit of criticism."

Was Mr. Schwab talking about carping criticism or about faultfinding? Of course not. He was talking about constructive, helpful criticism. He was talking about constructive, critical evaluation of the good as well as the bad. Artists have risen to greatness by critical appraisals of early efforts. Why not as much for salesmen? Why do salesmen not merit the competent, constructive criticism which may spur them to achieve greatness? And, who should be more competent to constructively criticize the work of a salesman than his sales manager?

Charles Schwab also said that he considered his ability to arouse enthusiasm in men his greatest asset. (Sales managers, please take note.) He also said that nothing else kills the ambition of men as criticism. Quickly, then, he added: "I am anxious to praise but loath to find fault." It seems that Mr. Schwab drew a clear line between carping criticism and constructive criticism. It also seems that he drew another line between criticism and faultfinding.

This is the area in which sales managers can personally profit. It is the area in which they can lift up their sales teams from average to superior ratings. It is the area in which they can make criticism their strong ally.

How is this to be done? Here are five ways:
1. Precede a critical observation with praise.

2. Use the "if I am wrong" approach.
3. Criticize by indirection. Use the "let me show you how we prefer to have it done because experience has taught us that it is the more profitable way for both of us." In this way criticism is coated with the sweetness of self-interest. It becomes more acceptable. It also becomes more effective than, "I can show you a better way." The latter implies that "you are wrong. I am right." This stiffens the necks of many listeners.
4. Remove the acid from criticism. Speak softly. Get across your point with a smile, or a laugh. Use yourself as the horrible example. Avoid embarrassing a member of your sales team.
5. In a person-to-person situation lavish justified praise on the one to whom you are speaking as a preamble to justified criticism. Thus criticism becomes less painful. You have recognized his good works. You have built him up. He is now less apt to resent merited criticism. You gave him a sense of importance. In this way you made criticism your strong ally instead of your enemy. Consequently you and your salesman shared in benefits of constructive criticism which had been stripped of pettiness so often associated with faultfinding.

In an effort to eliminate carelessness in detailed sales reports and orders, the sales manager of a pharmaceutical house assigned an offending salesman to make a talk at a sales meeting. The assigned subject: "How double-checking can clean up orders and sales reports." The result: The salesman made an informative talk. On his next trip into the territory his reports came back clean and his orders were without error. Errors in other salesmen's reports and orders were also reduced.

Principle: Criticism often can be made more effective by indirection than by faultfinding.

To stimulate his whole selling team the sales manager for a specialty food products distributor instituted a monthly sales-rating report for his selling team. It showed the relative standing of the salesmen. Two men on the team were the sales manager's target in this plan. Their volume had been consistently lagging. Result of publicity of their relative standings on the team brought up their volume. It also increased sales volume of all other salesmen on the team. This report, by indirection, became a persuasively critical method of nudging low-volume salesmen, and they responded constructively.

Distressed by the apparent loss of a substantial account the district sales manager for an advertising calendar production enterprise had summoned the accountable salesman to his office. The salesman breezed into the tense sales manager's office in a gay mood. Sternly the sales manager said: "You understand this isn't a social call. I want to talk to you about the way you handled the iron works account."

"Oh, that guy," the salesman responded. "He really blew his stack. He put the whole beef on you. I couldn't go for that so I straightened him out. I told him I goofed."

The sales manager's blood pressure went up. "He couldn't involve me in that mess. I wasn't to blame. But the sad part of it is that we lost the business. Doesn't that disturb you? Can't I get it across to you that we just can't afford to lose such accounts?"

"Who said we lost it?" the salesmen replied. "It's all settled. We got the business. It was quite simple. You see when I told him I was to blame he cooled off. We got together in fine shape. He even upped the size of his order about 50 per cent. You know that guy is really sold on calendar advertising and he's having a lot of fun panning me for making that blunder on his first order."

This salesman had shown his sales manager how vital it is to have all the facts before becoming critical. He also had demonstrated how to make criticism a sales-closing assist.

To make criticism a strong ally do this:

1. Devise ways to persuade salesmen to avoid or improve whatever you are criticizing.
2. Remove the acid from criticism by recognizing accomplishments of salesmen.
3. Project self-interest possibilities to inspire salesmen.
4. Strengthen your criticism of wrong doing by showing the right way to do it. Make the right way persuasively attractive.
5. Get the facts. Know your people and your problem. Cool your anger. Be constructive in criticism, and *persuasive.*

The Art of Face-Saving as a Sales Management Asset

The art of face-saving is the art of diplomacy in action. Isaac Goldberg, who wrote *The Wonder of Words,* had a keen insight into the meaning of the diplomatic art. Said Mr. Goldberg: "Diplomacy is to do and say the nastiest things in the nicest way."

You may disagree with Mr. Goldberg but there are few who will challenge the following definition of diplomacy: "Skill in dealing with others." The foregoing gets close to sales management.

Face-saving involves skill in dealing with others. It involves tact. This is closely related to the art of being constructively persuasive when we become critical.

Sir William Ostler maintained that "tact is the saving virtue without which no woman can be a success." For our purpose we might say that tact is the saving virtue in the art of face-saving and without it salesmen and sales managers are handicapped. It is a "fine instrument in the management of men."

The art of face-saving is an asset in sales management because:

1. *It involves* the dignity of every man on the sales team.
2. *It involves* personal importance.
3. *It involves* self-respect.
4. *It is* the art of providing "an out" for one caught in an embarrassing situation.
5. *It can be* "a fine instrument in the management of men."

Face-saving is the skill of critically calling attention to mistakes, or weaknesses, by indirection. In this method we reveal by example the seriousness of a blunder and allow time for the object lesson to penetrate the consciousness of the errant one.

Another device is to open the escape hatch for one unwittingly placed in an embarrassing situation. For example you might indicate agreement with the errant one to this extent: "You have a good point there," you say. "We should give that more thought." In his mind you have leaned toward his point of view. You now continue discussion on that phase of the issue on which you can agree. This develops the "yes" spirit. This is important in face-saving. You can now move more boldly into the delicate area where face-saving becomes vital. But, because you have preconditioned the errant one by persuasive reasoning to say "yes," he is yielding to your point of view. He does this without blushing. You have made it all possible by patience, tact, diplomacy and persuasion. You gained his confidence, your great asset in management of men.

Principle: Be constructively critical without finding fault.

Here is a tested formula for face-saving:

—Be diplomatic. Indirection, by example, is the tactful way to call attention to blunders or indiscretions.
—Make yourself the horrible example. Call attention to blunders you have made which he can identify with the blunder he has made. By admitting your own imperfections you have saved face for him.
—Give him an out. Ask questions which lead the one under criticism

to explain how it all happened. This provides him with a conscience-clearing escape from his embarrassing position. He finds a way to save face.

—Play down blunders. Make mistakes seem reasonably easy to repair. Magnify accomplishments. Play down the mishaps.

—Close a critical interview on a high note. Leave the erring one in a happy mood intent on improvement.

How to Make Rules Persuasive and Stimulators of Sales

To make sales management an orderly process we resort to rules. Experience has convinced us that the framework of a set of rules is desirable. This framework provides a basis for unity. It sets a standard for coordinated effort in the whole selling process.

The sales manager of a firm producing complex electronic equipment for business made this significant observation about rules: He said that whenever he was tempted to set up a new rule for his selling team he took note of the warning made by Voltaire that a multitude of laws is a sign of weakness. Rules, he said, were the laws by which his organization was governed. This sales manager also said that in establishing rules he heeded what Clarence Darrow once said: "Laws should be like clothes. They should be made to fit the people they are meant to serve."

Rules provide a selling team with a set of laws under which the entire organization can operate in an orderly manner. The dictionary calls a rule "a statement of what to do and what not to do; a law; a principal governing conduct."

The rule-making sales manager faces this problem: *How to make his rules produce more sales.* This requires that his rules must be so persuasive that salesmen comply with them. His rules must contain a motivating element which stimulates production by the sales team. His rules must be sufficiently persuasive to yield unified and enthusiastic response from the sales team. All this is quite necessary if rules are to become effective producers of sales.

Let us review rules in force in a variety of sales organizations. We find that they fall into three distinct classifications:

1. Restrictive Rules: These are the "thou shalt not" rules. They are designed to keep sales management and salesmen out of hot water. Whether such rules can cover the whole area of embarrassing situations is doubtful. It is suggested that before the restrictive rule goes into the book it be subjected to this searching question: "Will this rule stimulate or will it

hinder sales?" This brings into sharp focus the persuasive importance of the rule.

2. Punitive Rules: These are the "thou shalt not, or else" rules. In the first place they are restrictive. In the second place they establish either penalties for infractions of rules or imply that penalties will be imposed. It is difficult to imagine a stimulating rule which is based on punitive action. It is more difficult to discern persuasive power in punitive rules. Recognizing the book of rules as a sales stimulating tool, punitive rules should be approached with caution.

3. Helpful Rules: These are the "thou shalt" rules. They are established to inform, to encourage, to stimulate, to motivate salesmen. They point out areas for sales opportunity. They tell how to go about exploiting such areas and how to harmonize such effort with the over-all company policy. These rules are aimed directly at developing sales. They may include incentive rewards. Helpful rules are designed to build, not retard nor destroy. They are designed to lift up, not to knock down. They are designed to be persuasive, stimulating, and to make selling easier, not more difficult.

Representative books of rules cover such things as these:

(a) Dress—The persuasive selling power in neatness and appearance of the salesman.

(b) Conduct—The persuasive selling power in manners, courtesy, fairness, and conduct.

(c) Administration—Need for and the value to each salesman of unified procedure in report-making, handling complaints, and matters which require decision from higher authority.

(d) Sales Procedure—Such things as pricing, whether rigid or flexible, are covered under this rule. Limitations on making commitments on credit terms, on stocks available, or shipping dates come under this rule. This rule can be made a persuasive factor in selling by giving the salesmen specific policy requirements around which they can develop persuasive sales presentations.

"Reason is the life of the law," said Sir Edward Coke, famous English jurist. Reason, too, can be the life of rules in selling. This summons the judgment of sales management to establish persuasive *sales-making rules.*

Five Tested Ways of Teaching Salesmen How to Sell More

To be effective a sales manager's teaching methods must be persuasive. The art of persuasion and the art of being constructively critical are vitally important in teaching the new salesman to sell and in teaching the seasoned salesman to sell more.

Most of the successful sales managers have some knack for enlightening, encouraging, motivating and inspiring men to "reach for the sky" in selling. They have become skillful in criticizing performance without cutting a man down. They have become persuasive in their teaching and in their criticism.

Let us consider these five ways of teaching salesmen how to sell more:

Persuade Salesmen to Become Knowledgeable

Teach them to dig for facts about the products they sell. Teach them to search for new uses for those products. Impress upon them the profit possibilities in total knowledge of their products—how those products are made, how they can be used to benefit the buyer. Teach salesmen to know their territories, the people who live there, those who are in business there, their needs, their wants. Teach salesmen to search for clues to consumer demands. Teach them to gather facts about the economic capacity of the areas they serve.

The Critique Method of Teaching Salesmen to Sell

This is the art of being constructive and persuasive in criticism. Take an introductory session in your training program, for example. Mimeographed work sheets can be used for this purpose. Actual case record selling problems can be presented. The salesmen can be required to write on the work sheets how he proposes to approach this problem and effect a sale. The critique begins when the solutions are in. One by one the work sheets are discussed without mentioning names of salesmen. Student-salesmen are drawn into the discussion. In this way many shots are taken at the various suggested solutions. This participation can become constructively critical, for each salesman will recognize the case record on which he worked. During this participation the sales manager can critically appraise the new salesmen on their ability to think on their feet and handle themselves before an audience.

Show Them How to Do It

This is the graphic method. Use appropriate visual aids. Use the blackboard. Use pictures, graphs, maps, etc. Use motion picture strips whenever available. Tape recordings are also effective. The idea is to present selling techniques as graphically as possible. This, of course, is classroom training. Comparable training can be carried to salesmen in the field. Sales managers or designated training directors can profitably accompany salesmen on field trips where they can observe salesmen in action. They can conduct constructive and illuminating critiques at close of day in the privacy of a hotel room. There they can demonstrate and become persuasively critical, all with one purpose—to generate more persuasive and productive selling power.

The Post Mortem Training Method

These critiques are "after the fact" discussions. Many of these are highly productive. In these sessions salesmen relate their selling problems of the day. They tell how they handled tough situations. They give step-by-step accounts of how their presentations progressed, the objections encountered, and on to the close. They tell how they closed the sale or how they lost it. Each salesman profits by the experiences and thinking of his associates. The sales manager profits by getting an intimate glimpse of his selling team in action. New avenues for him to be helpful to the salesmen present themselves. A post mortem training session can be made constructively critical and persuasive.

Teach Salesmen How and When to Close

One sales manager who has a record of getting high sales production out of his staff said: "The knack of closing is a sixth sense. You develop a feeling for the right time to press for the close. It's difficult to teach anyone how or when to close."

These are five steps which have been tested and lead to sales. When skillfully followed, in order, these five steps have been sales producers. And, these five steps can be taught:

1. *Get attention.*
2. *Stimulate interest* and begin watching for "buying signals" from the prospect.
3. *Create desire* for what you have to sell. Suggest buying.
4. *Build up desire* to an eager want for what you have to sell. Ask for the order.

5. *It's buying time.* This is the action step. Press for a close.

The essence of effective selling is incorporated in the foregoing five steps. It is an uncomplicated, down-to-earth guide for sales training and for selling. It is flexible and adaptable for sales training programs designed to produce more sales.

How Persuasive Power in Plain Talk Creates Sales

A recruiting sergeant for the Marine Corps accomplished his selling mission by plain talk. He sold young men on the benefits to them of becoming "leathernecks." He accomplished this by refraining from the use of gobble-de-gook in his sales presentation. He gave it to them straight.

Dynamic sales managers "get through" to their selling teams with similar impact by plain talk. Dynamic salesmen sell more by relying on the convincing, persuasive power of plain talk.

Plain talk is endowed with five persuasive points. They are:
1. Plain talk is understandable.
2. Plain talk can be dramatically convincing.
3. Plain talk can have emotional appeal.
4. Plain talk can stimulate desire until desire becomes an irresistible want.
5. Plain talk holds attention because it is specific. It is down-to-earth communication. Plain talk is understandable, convincing and persuasive. It gets action. Plain talk *sells.*

Dynamic sales managers today are developing profitable sales volume by prying open communication channels with plain talk. They also do this:

Keep communication channels open with plain talk.
—Build persuasive selling teams with plain talk.
—Teach salesmen how to sell more through the art of plain talk.
—Motivate salesmen by plain talk to "reach for the sky" in selling.
—Criticize constructively and persuasively with plain talk.

These dynamic sales managers have experienced this fact: That plain talk is persuasive language. It promotes understanding. It overcomes objections. It achieves acceptance. It creates sales. It develops dynamic selling teams.

How Persuasive Power in Sharing Glory Yields High Rewards

For little more than two years a sales manager had occupied an uneasy position with a commercial property development enterprise.

However, his last 12 months turned out to be highly profitable. The executive board proposed a "victory dinner" to shower this sales manager with glory for his achievement. He countered with this suggestion:

"Thanks. By all means let's have a victory dinner. But, let's place the glory where it belongs—on the selling team we have developed. Let me tell the staff that they are men who put this program across. Let me tell them who are the top ten producers among them. Let me challenge them to aspire to a place on the top ten list. This is not my show. It belongs to the men who got out and wrote the business. All I did was train them."

The board agreed. The show went off as scheduled. The result: Sales volume began to climb at once and sustained its upward spiral. Why? Because a far-seeing sales manager saw the persuasive power in sharing glory.

Sales managers with vision neither anticipate nor wait for the executive board to make it convenient for them to share the glory of sales gains. They do it right along without fanfare. They recognize accomplishments in staff meetings, in sales conferences, at a luncheon, or they simply tell about how Jack or Fred has put over a real piece of selling. For instance, an introduction such as this is a powerful morale builder: "I want you to meet one of our newer salesmen. He has brought us some very desirable business in the few weeks he has been with us."

Principle: Accept compliments graciously. Then step out of the limelight and let the glory fall on the whole selling team. Express and show sincere appreciation for loyal team-work and for productive performance.

The Art of Being Persuasively Critical

Constructive criticism has these objectives: (a) to identify faults and errors; (b) to prevent repetition of such faults and errors.

Persuasive criticism has this objective: To crush all faults and errors by (a) identifying them; (b) by motivating others to correct or avoid such faults and errors.

The art of being persuasively critical is brought into focus by this brief dialogue between a sales manager and one of his salesmen:

SALES MANAGER: "I need your help. We have here a boner which occasionally causes us trouble. I believe you can give me an idea on how we can prevent this sort of mistake." (He explains the boner in detail.)

SALESMAN: "You know, Mr. Smith, I made a boner exactly like that one not more than a week ago. This is the way I got squared away on it." (He explains how he made out.)

SALES MANAGER: "Nice going, Joe. Do you think the way you

recognized your own mistake and squared it away, as you say, will prevent you from making that same mistake again?"

SALESMAN: "You can bet on that. Now that I have found out that others can flub a job, just as I did, I'll never fall into that trap again."

In the foregoing dialogue we see how a sales manager can get across the seriousness of a mistake without bruising a salesman. By indirection the sales manager *persuaded* the salesman to become more alert. He *persuaded* the salesman to become self-critical. He *persuaded* the salesman to vow that he would avoid such blunders in the future. And the persuasiveness of the sales manager was so artfully camouflaged that the erring salesman believed he was the author of the corrective idea.

Test these five keys to persuasive criticism:

1. Make faults seem easy to correct or avoid.
2. Condemn the fault, not the blunderer.
3. Stimulate self-criticism to minimize errors.
4. Avoid crushing initiative by trying to crush mistakes. Lloyd Jones put it this way: "The men who try to do something and fail are infinitely better than those who try to do nothing and succeed."
5. Motivate salesmen to "reach for the sky" in error-free performance as well as in selling.

chapter 9

How to Improve Public Relations for the Sales Force by Persuasive Selling

Let us assume that one of your salesmen is at this moment in face-to-face contact with a prospect or a customer. He's your ambassador. What sort of impression is he making? Does he make friends easily? Do they stay with him? Do they believe in him? Do his contacts confide in him? Does he win the confidence of those to whom he sells?

Now let us suppose that you attempt to show that salesman how he can improve his relationship with prospects and customers. What then? Many sales managers do this persuasively. Their salesmen see the need, and the benefit to them, of improved public relations. They respond favorably. Thus a chain reaction is set in motion and it yields high dividends. He may hit the jackpot. In that case both he and you benefit. Your entire sales force benefits by being motivated to go and do likewise. But you, the sales manager, are out front as a beneficiary in your salesman's public relations success.

You taught that salesman *how* the art of public relations contributes to selling more goods and services.

You taught him that good will requires constant cultivation. Unless it is nourished it withers.

You taught him that the key to persuasive power is sincerity.

You taught him that when persuasion in selling is followed by more persuasion the result is more sales.

You taught him that customer welfare, service, communication, integrity and overall integrity are the ingredients of productive persuasive salesmanship.

The glow of success which now shines on your salesman also glows on you as his sales manager. It also reflects brightly upon the house you and your salesman represent. Moreover, it casts a favorable light on your whole selling team.

Persuasive selling can become a dynamic force in public relations. The good-will-building factor in persuasive selling stimulates sales volume. It lays a foundation for doing business on pleasant terms. It removes drudgery from work. It promotes mutual understanding.

This may appear to be a new role for the art of persuasion in selling, but it is not. The pioneer wagon salesman capitalized on this art. He probably knew little about such terms as public relations and persuasion. Nevertheless he did develop skill in making and holding friends and in selling goods. The same principle is applicable to the market today. However, we have become more aggressive than the wagon salesman. A competitive spirit nudges us to sell more. To meet this challenge the sales manager has the responsibility of improving public relations for the sales force. To achieve this objective he uses persuasive selling as his main vehicle. He teaches his selling team how to improve public relations through more persuasive power in their sales presentations.

In this, the challenge to sales management is, in itself, persuasive. It can also become exceedingly profitable for you as a sales manager and for each member of your selling team.

Sales Manager's Role in Favorable Public Relations

Public relations, as it relates to the selling team, can be defined in this way:

The technique used by individuals to establish favorable attitudes and develop favorable responses from individuals or groups.

In the majority of cases attitudes and responses are the products of persuasion. For instance: A jewelry salesman decided to get training in public speaking. For him, this developed greater persuasive power in his sales presentations. In time this carried him to a sales manager's position. There he distinguished himself in two ways: (a) As a persuasive leader—he inspired and motivated salesmen; (b) as a tactful, persuasive executive.

He developed favorable relationships with his staff and with the higher executive echelon in the organization. He also extended his skill in public relations to customers and prospective customers. This skillful merchant of gems and jewelry relied on his persuasive power to improve public relations for his selling team.

To make progress in improving public relations for sales forces, far-seeing sales managers tighten their grasp on the art of persuasion in selling. Try these three keys for opening doors to advancement in favorable public relations:

1. Develop skill in clear-cut communication.
2. Become a better listener. Persuade others to unburden their minds.
3. Talk about the other man's problems. Concentrate on helping him solve his problems. Become more persuasive by talking about benefits for him.

In developing a productive selling team the sales manager stakes his success on his ability to effectively communicate. Training salesmen requires teaching which inspires and motivates. It is more than setting up charts showing how it should be done. Motivation and inspiration require an answer to the question in the salesman's mind: "Why should I do it this way?" This is where the art of persuasion in sales management is challenged. Persuasion means influencing. Effective persuasion is also convincing.

In a sales seminar one executive passed out questionnaires to his sales force. This was an evaluation quiz. He wanted to know just how well he stacked up in the eyes of the men he directed. He asked for no signatures on the quiz sheets. As a result he received blunt answers to his questions. Here is a digest of a few pertinent replies he received:

One salesman described his sales manager as "arrogant."

One salesman said he expected a sales manager to "give him a lift," but, instead, he said the sales manager made him angry. This man was looking for motivation. He probably realized he was weak but he wanted to improve.

One man refused to complete the questionnaire. He said he didn't trust the sales manager.

The sales manager was described as a "poker-faced listener" by one man. This man said he felt that the sales manager's mind was already made up before a discussion began. For this reason he thought it was useless to present any of his problems.

One man wrote: "The gang feels that your communication line has broken down."

Another man wrote: "A lot of us would like you to level with us."

One man wrote: "Everything is not well in our territory. We hear a lot of gripes from the public. We don't feel free to bring these unpleasant things to you. Why don't you open the door, or do you just want bouquets?"

This sales manager evaluated his effort to find out more about the thinking of his selling team: "I believe it was the most effective step I have ever taken as an executive. I looked into every one of those bricks that were thrown at the sales manager's office. Most of them had real substance. What good did this do? I went to work at once to clear the atmosphere. Misunderstanding has given way to freedom of expression. As a result this selling team is doing a bang-up job in their field in public relations as well as in selling."

Persuasive Ways to Blow Your Own Horn

The principle involved in "blowing your own horn" is simply this: *Expose yourself in a favorable, persuasive light.*

The public relations counselor for a chain of banks once put it this way: "To sell banking service you have to get through with your story to key people. You can do legitimate horn blowing. But you have to keep in tune with the attitudes and needs of those you aspire to draw into your client network."

Consider these three persuasive ways in which sales management can "blow its own horn":

1. *Unusual Sales Gains.* Make a great show of it. Give the sales team credit for scoring this gain. Be justifiably proud to be associated with such a gingery group of business-builders.

2. *Special Recognition.* In the military and naval services they decorate a man for outstanding performance. Why not a salesman? Why not turn the spotlight on a high-scoring salesman? Tell the sales team how he first came to the team. Tell the salesmen how he has contributed to the total sales volume. Perhaps there will be more than one of these outstanding performers. In any case, you, the sales manager will be right there with them to present them, their records, and their honors. Part of the glow will reflect on you as you pin an achievement award on a salesman's lapel.

3. *Bonus Time.* This is a natural for horn blowing. The sales manager reviews the steps that have been taken to improve selling techniques and public relations through persuasive selling. He reiterates the incentives that have been offered

for sales increases. He reviews special recognition awards that have been made for outstanding performance. All this leads up to the pay-off: The bonus. Such "horn blowing" is gleefully accepted by the sales team. But, it's persuasive horn-blowing, too. Bonus payments, made with a flourish, can be made most persuasive and effective and contribute mightily to internal public relations.

Some sales managers use their own living rooms as sounding boards for their ideas. There they can "blow their own horns." If their wives are constructively critical they can save their men much pain and embarrassment. In their adroit, feminine way some wives have mastered the art of cutting an unduly boastful husband down to size. Discerning wives usually are more outspoken than salesmen on the sales force when it comes to aiming a shot at the sales manager. However, wives and salesmen have a tendency to draw a distinction between bragging and persuasive horn blowing. The distinction is this:

(a) Bragging, or boasting, is self-praise. It is the "How great I am" approach. It shoves the braggart into the spotlight and pushes his victims (the listeners) out of the picture. Thus, a fertile breeding ground is prepared for ill will, bad public relations.

(b) The persuasive horn-blower is more subtle. If he is a sales manager he takes his selling team, or a selected salesman, to the center of the stage. Around the selling team, or the singled-out salesman he weaves his web. He promotes his idea. He sells his product or his strategy. He glorifies the salesmen as the real producers, not himself. This is the persuasive way to "blow your own horn."

Principle: For effective horn-blowing tune in with a note of self-interest for those you aim to influence by persuasive horn-blowing.

The Market Potential in Good Will

Good will is the *intangible assets* of a business as reflected in *prestige,* and *friendly relations with customers.*

Is this intangible asset marketable? Does it have dollar-value? It is not only marketable but it has a price tag on it.

The market potential of good will can be illustrated by the principle of an old, yet well-tested, rule in salesmanship: "Don't argue with a prospect. You may win the argument, but you may also lose the sale." You may also destroy that intangible asset called good will.

The foregoing rule ties a sale to good will and thereby establishes a certain price tag on good will.

In a panel discussion at an industrial conference the following principle won wide support among the participants: No business can afford to allow its reputation or its product to be misunderstood or distrusted. This principle places wide responsibilities upon sales management.

It is not uncommon to read of a business offered for sale with the selling price based on two factors: (a) physical assets; (b) good will. Nor is it uncommon to close such a sale with more paid for the good will than for the physical assets.

Sales management learns through constant contact with fickle buyers that good will, while being an intangible, has a high market potential.

Good will can be built up and it can be knocked down by the members of selling teams in such areas as these:

1. *Friendship.* Selling volume is more secure when friendly customer relationships prevail. Sales have a tendency to drop off when friendship between buyer and seller cools.
2. *Prestige.* A solid foundation for favorable public relations can be built upon prestige. Selling teams can do much to maintain the prestige of the house they represent. They can also destroy that intangible asset by negative acts or thoughtlessness.
3. *Faith.* When confidence in a product or in a business enterprise runs high in the market place the dollar-value of good will becomes evident. Such faith is subject to the perils of poor public relations policy. By the same token, this faith, this good-will confidence, is strengthened when persuasive selling is associated with awareness of the intangible value of good will.

Sales management can fire up selling teams to drive through obstacles to reach the productive heart of a market area. It can do this by developing confidence in its product and by establishing prestige in the market area. Those are the intangibles we call "good will" and "favorable public relations." In many instances such intangibles dominate great sales exploitations. The market potential of good will provides a continuing challenge to persuasive sales management. A thoughtless act by a salesman can harden sales resistance. Indifference in the home office to customer problems can lose sales. That's the price tag which good will carries.

—On the Constructive Side: A well-timed friendly letter can create good will and open gates to new riches in the market place.
—On the Constructive Side: A thoughtful act by a salesman can break down sales barriers and admit him into fertile gardens where sales grow in abundance.

—On the Constructive Side: Quick, positive, helpful response to complaints from the field can build sales. Such action reflects interest in customer attitudes and problems. In the climate thus created prestige thrives, and the market potential of good will becomes a reality. The ultimate result shows up on the sales graph.

Favorable public relations requires that it must be fostered, promoted and earned. No department is more favorably situated to contribute to favorable public relations than the sales department. The selling team has been, or should be persuaded to go after business by persuasive selling. That same selling team can improve public relations by the same power which produces sales—the art of persuasion.

It was Socrates who gave us a simple guiding principle for building good will. He said: "The shortest and surest way to live with honor in the world is *to be in reality what we appear to be.*"

Why the Best Salesmen Are Image-Makers

Salesmen are saddled with the responsibility of being image-makers. The impressions they make in their contacts have a direct effect on sales management. Every day they are testing how well they have been indoctrinated by sales managers in the value of favorable public relations and its relationship to the art of persuasive salesmanship.

Public relations has become the "in" thing. Professional people have become aroused to its worth. Lawyers and doctors are striving to improve their relationship with clients and patients. Giant corporations are aware of the value of this intangible asset in business. Industrial enterprises are contributing huge sums to education, to charitable institutions, to health and to hospitals. All this for one purpose: To improve the corporate image.

One discerning corporate executive has pointed out this fact which stresses the importance of public relations to the selling team: He asserts that the average person, either in business or in private life, usually passes judgment on the house he or she deals with by contact with a single individual. In the majority of cases that individual is a salesman. His conduct is the product of some sales manager's training system.

But, let us understand this thing we call "image-making." It is the creation of clear mental pictures in the minds of customers and potential customers. Those clear mental pictures should be favorable, for our purpose. Basically, then, the salesman has a three-point responsibility in this matter:

1. *To create a favorable self-image.* By his appearance, his neatness, his speech, his manners, his general conduct, he is

obligated to make a favorable impression on prospective buyers.

2. *To create a favorable image of the house he represents.* This he can also do by personal conduct. Similarly through his self-image he can contribute to the stature of his superiors and to the reputation of the house he and the executive staff represent.

3. *To create a favorable product-image.* This he can best do by showing (through convincing evidence) how the product he sells can benefit those who buy it and use it.

It is apparent from the forgoing that the self-image of a salesman carries a heavy burden. But sales managers, too, must share in this responsibility. They, too, are image-makers in their own sphere.

Seven creative steps, when taken by sales managers, can lead their selling teams toward improvement in public relations by persuasive selling. Let us consider those seven steps:

1. Create a favorable *executive image* to favorably impress the selling teams.

2. Create a favorable *public image* to favorably impress those who are directly contacted by their salesmen.

3. Create a favorable *teaching image* to become more persuasively effective in training sales teams.

4. Create a favorable *team image* to develop unity and pride in the selling team.

5. Create an alluring *image of a product* to accent its salability. This to motivate the selling team to sell more persuasively.

6. Create a favorable *house image,* stressing stability, products produced and/or sold, and capacity to advance the interests of its patrons. This requires in-depth knowledge and understanding of policies for maximum selling impact. Herein sales management can upgrade the firm, its products and its personnel. All this involves image-making on a broad scale with high stakes for sales management.

7. Create a factual *image of rewards* available to the selling team for improving public relations and for more persuasive selling. The objective: To motivate salesmen to become better image-makers and to "reach for the sky" in selling.

How to Sell Public Relations to Your Staff

The sales manager of a woolen mills operation who directs a force of sales people selling directly to consumers and another group selling to tailors and the retail trade, places public relations on his top priority list for sales meeting discussions.

"Salesmen have a tendency to discount the value of public relations," he said. "Some growl that you can't sell goods by sweet-talking customers, or by being a do-gooder. From this I judge that public relations rates low in the estimation of sales people. For this reason I attack the problem on the basis that it is an unpopular subject. When I call a salesman to my office among the first questions I shoot at him are these: 'How are you making out with Mr. Jones? He turned sour on us for a time, didn't he? What have you done to sweeten his mood?'

"The answers to such questions usually bring out the attitude of a salesman toward public relations. This gives me the clue to what I will have to do to make that salesman more effective.

"In a group sales meeting my agenda usually begins with a specific point in public relations which has proved to be profitable for salesmen. I also try to wind up a meeting with a reminder that it is more pleasant and also more profitable to sell on a friendly basis."

One evidence that a salesman is making progress in favorable public relations is when a customer recommends the salesman, the house, or the product, or all three, to someone not on your customer list.

To convert your sales team to an all-out public relations effort the best approach is by the art of persuasion. This is a three-step process:

1. Appeal to a salesman's self-interest. Thereby you get attention. You arouse interest and desire. Present factual evidence of how favorable public relations has paid off for other salesmen.

2. Explain how smiles pay off. Smile as you make this presentation. This is the art of persuasion at work. Persuade salesmen to close sales with a note of enthusiasm about the advantage of the deal to the buyer. Convince your salesmen that by closing a sale with a spirit of good fellowship the door is left open for the next call.

3. Teach the persuasive power in the "hello" greeting. Too many salesmen call only when they want to sell something. Too few stop in to just say, "hello." On the other hand, sales are often killed by undue familiarity. Those who profit most by friendliness know their people. They know when it is well to say "hello." It is amazing how often a friendly call, made just to say, "hello," leads to shop talk. Some beautiful· orders have been written in such informal calls.

Teach salesmen to maintain tactful, friendly contacts with prospective buyers. Teach them to be observant. Teach them to detect opportunities to be of service to a customer or a prospective customer. Teach them the art of considerate courtesy. Teach them that this is persuasive selling with a dynamic public relations punch included.

The most effective way for sales management to sell public relations to the selling team is by the "hard sell." Begin by creating a more persuasive self-image for yourself. Follow this by: (a) arousing curiosity, then interest in public relations as a selling force; (b) creating desire for more knowledge of the friendship angle for doing more business; (c) showing how other salesmen have profited by "friendship selling"; (d) defining the difference between solid public relations effort and confidence-destroying "apple polishing."

There is nothing complicated, or mysterious, or flimsy about public relations. It is a near relative to friendliness. Public relations simply takes friendliness into the market place. Salesmen can be taught how to become skillful in public relations just as they can be taught how to improve their sales technique by mastering the art of persuasion. After all, this is the major selling assignment for sales management.

How to Turn Complaints into Public Relations Opportunities

Someone once said: "The man who complains reveals his interest." Sales management might paraphrase this statement in this way: "The man who cares enough to complain cares enough to be sold."

A sales manager in the carpet industry thumped his desk one morning and sounded off to a group of his salesmen. He said: "Most of the complaints you have brought to me from your territories are most encouraging to me. Most of them appear to me to be invitations to you to do a more thorough selling job with those people. Those who complained have simply let the bars down for you. If you had been on your toes when they complained to you I wonder if you could not have moved in and written some business. Let me ask you: What did you do to set these complaining customers right? Couldn't you have said: 'I believe you have a good point there. Let me tell you what we are doing in that very direction.' Had you even so much as hinted that you had an idea which could pay off for them they would have forgotten about their gripes and listened to you."

The salesman who has mastered the art of persuasion can go a long way toward cooling off complainants.

For Salesmen: Complaints often provide opportunities for them to become persuasive and turn the complaints into sales commitments. The technique is similar to turning sales resistance into selling points.

For Sales Management: Complaints often reveal the strength and also the weaknesses in the selling team. In backing up salesmen who are under pressure from unhappy accounts, sales managers may discover how well their salesmen have mastered the art of persuasion. In doing this sales managers also become more intimately acquainted with those who buy what they have to sell.

Complaints may also disclose strong and weak points in sales management's training program. After troubled waters have been calmed it is good public relations policy to make the customer feel rewarded for complaining. If this is accomplished sales management and the salesman profit by the experience. Selling in all its phases must be persuasive. And this, of course, includes the knack of making a gripe pay off in good will and future business.

Enduring success in public relations invariably is based on sincerity of purpose. The objective in improving public relations for the sales force is to build and strengthen a climate of friendship for selling. The purpose: To promote more persuasive selling.

chapter 10

How to Soothe Trouble Spots in Sales Management by the Art of Persuasion

"Trouble is the spice which gives zest to sales management," said a dynamic sales manager to a group of his executive colleagues who had been amazed by his zeal in tackling problems which they were inclined to evade.

To support his position this sales manager pointed out what Robert Updegraff, a perceptive publisher, had said: "Be thankful for the troubles of your job . . . . If it were not for the things that go wrong, the difficult people you have to deal with . . . someone could be found to handle your job for half what you are being paid."

That sales manager and also that publisher acknowledged that trouble can be a constructive force. Trouble, with its attendant problems, is closely related to the responsibilities of sales management. Dynamic sales managers accept trouble as a challenge, rather than as a burden. By this attitude they become master problem-solvers and persuasive trouble-shooters. They are open-minded men. They are willing to admit that trouble can result from executive bungling as well as from errors of subordinates. They are persuasive executives. The challenge which fascinates them is the problem of soothing trouble spots.

Various sources of troubles which plague sales managers have been identified. Among them are: (a) bad judgment, (b) temper, (c) indifference.

Regardless of the nature of trouble which "bugs" sales managers, and regardless of the source of that trouble, it won't vanish, nor will it go away simply because we ignore it. Trouble has tenacious adhesive qualities. Perhaps this is why trouble is so challenging to so many dynamic sales executives. Henry Ward Beecher, noted clergyman, put his finger on one challenging point prevalent in trouble, and which may often be overlooked. He said: "Troubles are often the tools by which God fashions us for better things."

In sales management there are three primary sources from which most troublesome problems arise: (1) people, (2) communications, (3) objectives.

Suppose we pull these trouble sources apart to get a clear idea of what sales management is up against:

People as a Trouble Source

A sales manager's first problem is to recruit a competent sales team. To challenge him someone drops a document on his desk which discloses that only 5% of some 70 graduates from a well recognized college have expressed the slightest interest in selling as a career. He could throw up his hands in despair, but he doesn't. Instead he determines to get his share of those who are seriously interested in selling as a career. But, when he does get them he also gets problems. He anticipated that. They must be trained. He must develop the team spirit in them. He must also infect them with selling fever. When this is done he is not free of trouble. He still has people to contend with. Potential customers must be persuaded to buy his product. This expands his troubles, but it enlarges his challenge.

Solution: To develop more persuasive selling all the way from sales management to salesmen, from salesmen to the buyers.

Communication as a Trouble Source

Misunderstanding lurks in the wings to make trouble for sales management. Misunderstanding can result from lack of clarity in speech, in writing a memorandum or a letter, in face-to-face communication, and also in telephone conversation. The danger of double-meaning exists and has potent trouble-making power. A veteran editorial writer had a unique method of assuring himself that what he had written would be understood as he intended it to be. He would ask a copy boy to read what he had written. Then he would ask the copy boy to tell him what he had just read. This seasoned editor explained: "If that kid can understand what I have written then perhaps our readers will get the point." He was striving for clarity because he wanted to be persuasive.

Solution: Clarity first. Then persuasive action to clear up misunderstanding.

Objectives as Trouble Spots

Lack of agreement on plans and purposes lies at the bottom of most of these difficulties. Again, this involves people. It also ties in with communication. Total understanding of policy and methods is involved.

Solution: Clarify your objectives. Be specific and persuasive. Be understood.

Persuasive power is that which influences. It can and does soothe trouble spots for sales managers. It has great strength in its simplicity. It is simply the art of winning over. It is the art of being convincing. And, it is the art of being understood in what you say and what you write. The art of persuasion is a major tool for dynamic sales management.

Four Nagging Problems and How Persuasion Helps Solve Them

Let's face it, seasoned sales managers rarely anticipate a pleasant day. To most of them a trouble-free day would be somewhat boring. By anticipating the unexpected and alerting themselves to deal with emergency situations those sales managers make themselves great in their respective fields. They are seldom caught off guard.

Consider now these four problems which constantly nag sales managers and require constructive action:

Manpower

Before a sales manager can get into action he must assemble a selling team. In recruiting this team he searches for men who are dedicated to salesmanship. If they are not so dedicated but appear to have the necessary qualifications, the sales manager turns to persuasive power to instill within those men that spirit of dedication which is desired. By persuasion he convinces candidates for the selling team that they have the capacity to achieve greatness in selling. He tells them why he believes they have this qualification. By demonstrating his faith in them he becomes persuasive. Turnover is a troublesome and costly manpower problem. Persuasion has, in many cases, cooled off the greener pasture fever and diverted attention of salesmen to the opportunities existing in the job at hand.

Principle: Bolster the team spirit through the art of persuasion. Bolster personal pride of accomplishment in selling through the art of persuasion. Stimulate creative thinking and initiative through the art of persuasion. The power in persuasive selling can build sales volume and it can also develop selling power in the sales team.

Attitude

The nagging problem of developing the right attitude has two faces—the sales manager's own attitude and the overall attitude of the selling team. Some sales managers, for instance, hold back instead of driving ahead. Fear in some form usually is at the bottom of this attitude. One industrial leader detected this attitude in his organization. "I had to take drastic action with my sales manager," he said. "He was a good planner, a creative, imaginative man. He got along well with his staff, but he was fearful that his men might make a mistake. His fearfulness killed initiative in some of our best salesmen." Sales managers find it profitable to develop initiative, courage, and persuasive power in their salesmen. One distinguished business executive said, "Becoming outstanding at anything is largely a matter of attitude." The question then arises: "How can we change an attitude?" It has been accomplished in two ways: (a) by self-persuasion, (b) by persuading others to look at a problem optimistically, constructively, and even persuasively.

Principle: Positive, persuasive action encourages constructive attitudes. It fosters pride in accomplishment, initiative and unity in the selling team. It discourages buck-passing for below-standard performance by placing a premium on exceptional performance.

Salesmanship

To develop a team of master salesmen is the dream of most sales managers. It, too, has its nagging problems. Most of these problems can be solved by (a) mastering the art of persuasion in selling and by applying this art in sales management as well as in selling goods and services. Through the art of persuasion selling teams have been and can be encouraged to "reach for the sky" in selling; and, (b) by employing the power of persuasion to combat negative thinking, to show how positive action reaps the harvest for the selling team.

Principle: Through the art of persuasion in sales management as well as in the selling team, record-breaking sales volume can be achieved. The art of persuasion travels well in double harness.

Sales Resistance

Four ghosts haunt some salesmen. They introduce these phantom-like barriers to sales to their disappointed sales managers, thus multiplying sales management's troubles. You may recognize some of these ghosts: (a) "The trouble is. . . .", and the excuse for falling down on a sale goes on and on in that vein. (b) "He'll probably buy tomorrow," and giving no thought to the fact that tomorrows are always in the indefinite future. (c) "I'll try, but it probably won't work." A self-conditioning ghost has been working on this salesman. This ghost specializes on failures. (d) "Dealers don't have any call for anything in my line. . . ." In that statement the alert sales manager sees a clue that his salesman has neglected to show one more prospect how he could profit by creating demand for one or more items in the line.

Sales resistance is a rolling stone. It may originate with the consumer, roll on to the dealer, flare up for the salesman, and be pushed on for a solution to the sales manager. This trail does not lead to reducing sales resistance. It may even foster it. The foundation for sales volume is laid at the same spot where sales resistance begins. The foundation for sales volume is constructed out of the ingredients in persuasive selling, which are the ingredients used effectively for combating sales resistance. The art of persuasion is the vitamin that puts energy in the blood stream of salesmen.

A sales manager in the fashion field explained how he handles sales resistance. "I tell my men frankly that they are up against tough competition and stubborn sales resistance. This, in one blow, kills any spark of the easy-life attitude which might be alive in the salesmen. I try to stir them up to sell in a tough market. I pay a bonus when they land a much-wanted and hard-to-get account. But the account must measure up to those specifications."

Principle: The ingenuity of sales management is challenged in applying the power of persuasion. But, persuade we must, if we would sell, profitably, and in volume.

In the number one problem of sales management, which is man-power, and the training of men to sell, Sir Leslie Stevens once passed on this bit of wisdom from which sales managers might profit:

"The only way in which one human being can properly attempt to influence another is by encouraging him to think for himself, instead of endeavoring to instill ready-made opinions into his head."

The Pay-Off in Persuasive Trouble-Shooting

The general manager of a retail merchandising operation with several branch outlets was pleased with his new sales manager. He said: "That fellow is a whiz at trouble-shooting. He makes trouble-shooting pay off in a big way."

Sales management, too, can enjoy the fruits of persuasive trouble-shooting in such areas as these:

1. By changing negative attitudes of problem salesmen to positive action. Doing this, tangible profits accrue to the salesmen and also to sales management.
2. By cooperating with salesmen in developing skills for getting through to tough prospects and then, by persuasion, breaking down sales resistance.
3. By soothing trouble spots through the art of persuasion by (a) settling disputes and differences among salesmen; (b) by settling disputes and differences between sales management and salesmen; (c) by promoting accord and settling differences between customers and salesmen. (In each of the foregoing areas the stakes are high enough to challenge sales management's most persuasive efforts.)

Barnhart defines a trouble-shooter as one who *discovers* and *eliminates* causes of trouble. This elevates trouble-shooting to a constructive status.

For the sales manager who, by the very nature of his position, is required to function as a trouble-shooter, the Barnhart definition suggests at least three required qualifications—inquisitiveness, discernment, and persuasiveness. Inquisitiveness will motivate him to probe the source and the nature of trouble. Discernment will enable him to see signs of trouble, even in time to avert catastrophe. The art of persuasion can enable him to smoothly rectify errors, misunderstandings and other matters falling into the trouble slot.

After rating his sales manager as "a whiz at trouble-shooting" the retail merchandising executive rates ability and willingness to delegate responsibility next in importance. "Other men on the staff may be better research men," he said. "They may be better investigators, or better probers for hidden sources of trouble. Good sales management requires that such talent be recognized and used to increase the tangible pay-off."

Other recognized requirements for trouble-shooting sales managers are these:

Patience—Instead of exploding the patient sales manager capitalizes on errors. He patiently reasons with balky customers. By persuasion he leads them to see a problem from two points of view—the customer's and his own. By patience he soothes trouble spots and enjoys a higher pay-off.

Knowledge—By acquiring technical knowledge of products, knowledge of market problems, and knowledge of buyers' problems the trouble-shooting sales manager is in position to team up with salesmen in soothing trouble spots as they occur, often before they occur. He also becomes better qualified to increase sales volume through the art of persuasion.

Understanding—Sales managers might profit by heeding this biblical admonition: "Wisdom is the principal thing; therefore get wisdom: and with all thy getting get understanding." Sympathetic understanding of men, their aspirations, their problems, their strengths and their weaknesses is vital in sales management. It becomes an asset in trouble-shooting, where it promises higher pay-off. Equally important is the vitality of understanding in motivation, in team effort, in the overall objective of persuasion in sales management which is to attain more persuasive selling for greater sales volume.

Sales managers, being constantly in working harness with salesmen, have two types of personalities with which to contend: (1) the objective type, who work best with others; and (2) the subjective type, who work best with themselves. How skillfully have you assigned each member of your sales staff? Is he in a spot best suited to his personality? Or, could the pay-off for him and for you be increased by reassignment? Have you also analyzed yourself? Are you the objective or the subjective type? Could you increase the pay-off and perhaps reduce the necessity for trouble-shooting by delegating more responsibilities to others who may be better adapted by personality to soothe the trouble spots?

"With all your getting get understanding!"

How to Uncover the Basis of Sales Resistance

I knew a sales manager who enjoyed sales resistance. On the slightest indication that his selling team was slowed down by a sales barrier in any area of his territory he became recharged with a new zeal for selling. He became more convincing. He became more persuasive. Moreover, he expected his salesmen to also get aroused by the sales resistance. He maintained that sales resistance was a lame excuse for letting down on selling. It ought to be a tonic, not a sedative, he said.

One day this sales manager received a report of strong sales resistance. He struck out at once to uncover the basis of that sales barrier. He insisted on getting out where the action was. "How can you combat something until you can see it?" he asked. "How can you attack sales resistance until you find the source of that opposition? I'll give you the answer to that question," he said. "You've got to get to the bottom of the problem."

Inquisitiveness is an asset in sales management. Inquisitiveness can also be persuasive. For example, it can drive a sales manager to probe and to find out about the source of sales resistance so he can put up a fight against it.

An inquisitive sales manager, challenged by sales resistance, activates what we might call the "Three P" formula. This is it: (1) Perception, (2) Patience, (3) Persuasion.

With this formula as a guide the sales manager can move ahead with confidence. He can fix his objective in the following areas which are all related to sources of sales resistance:

1. The Salesman: He is the No. 1 target in sales resistance. He is on the front line where the resistance is the hottest. Resistance may come from: (a) a troublesome prospect or an upset customer; (b) a dealership where buying is stalled because too many people in the organization have a hand in buying and marketing policy; (c) territorial disinterest in the product or service.

2. The Territory: The big question here is: What regional characteristic, what peculiarities in the market, what difficulties are there in supplying the needs and the wants of the people in this area, and how are all these factors affecting sales and why? Your problem as sales manager: To uncover and identify all obstacles to full-scale selling. To determine why these obstacles exist. To determine how they can be removed or neutralized. Then remove them or neutralize them so you and your selling team can get on with the business of building profitable sales volume.

3. Competition: If competition is hot it may well stimulate interest in buying as well as in selling. How does your competition react to sales resistance? If competition is skimming off the cream of the business in the market where your selling team has advised you that sales resistance is formidable then you do have a sizeable trouble-shooting job on your hands. Somewhere in your selling team a weakness exists. Find it. Restore that persuasive power which is now lacking and sales resistance will probably decline.

Sales resistance has a realistic base. At times salesmen have been known to magnify the loss of a much-desired sale into area-wide sales resistance. In other cases failure to observe or to be sufficiently persuasive has lost a sale and this has been described as sales resistance. Consider this actual case record. It reveals how sales resistance can be misinterpreted:

Salesman "A" reported that his top prospect for the day was a "dud." "Calendar advertising is out," the prospect insisted. The calendar salesman assured his sales manager that he produced evidence of increasing use of calendars in the prospect's own line of business. This failed to persuade the prospect to seriously consider this medium. The inquisitive sales manager made a personal trip to the prospect's place of business. There he saw calendars on walls in every office in this prospect's establishment. He also saw desk calendars in use. In the prospect's private office the visiting sales manager saw a calendar on the wall advertising the prospect's competitor. There he saw opportunity for selling calendars for advertising purposes. The prospect's walls testified that he was favorable to commercial calendars. The sales manager had pin-pointed the source of sales resistance, however. It was in the mind of his own salesman. This simplified the sales manager's problem. That prospect became a user of calendar advertising.

Principle: Get to the bottom of sales resistance whenever and wherever it shows up. Determine its nature. Determine its source. Take prompt and positive remedial action. Such trouble spots often yield to constructive and persuasive action.

The Art of Persuasion in Making Decisions

When trouble spots are exposed it is up to sales management to make a decision. Some of us do this by "snap judgment." Others mull over a problem. They look at it from every angle before arriving at a decision. Some seek counsel. In all but "snap judgment" the art of persuasion enters into decision making.

Problems of sales management can affect the whole selling team. In such instances this question comes up: "Would two heads be better than one?" If we agree that more than one should be involved in decision making then we try to reach accord. This brings the art of persuasion prominently into the picture.

One sales manager I knew had become known for his problem-solving ability. When he was asked how he tackled a problem he replied: "Go in with an open mind. No fixed notions." I overheard him in an important problem-solving meeting. These were the steps he took to achieve his objective: (a) He aroused interest in his proposed solution. (b) He supplemented his solution with suggested solutions he had received from his salesmen. (c) He went over each proposal point by point, eliminating one after another until only two proposals were left before him and his assistant. (d) In open debate they arrived at a unanimous decision on one of the two proposals. (e) He submitted the plan to his salesmen and they bought it.

The key to that sales manager's success was good salesmanship. He settled a troublesome problem by getting mutual accord. He achieved this result by a four-step presentation to his selling team:

1. He opened up with a point on which he was quite sure all would agree.
2. He followed this with another point on which general accord was reasonably certain.
3. On these two points he got unanimous approval with affirmative action on each point separately. In doing this he was developing the "yes" attitude in the group.
4. He introduced the vital point at issue and promptly brought it to a vote. He secured unanimous approval on this solution primarily because he had created in four steps a spirit of accord in the group. This was persuasion in action.

Sales management is charged with the responsibility of making decisions through which profitable sales volume may be developed. Hopefully, the sales manager is also given executive power to put such decisions into effect.

Decision making is briefly defined as "the making up of one's mind." This may be over-simplification. Decision making is not always easy. As Elbert Hubbard, the publisher and author, who presided over "The Roycrofters" in East Aurora, New York, saw it: "It does not take much strength to do things, but it takes great strength to decide on what to do."

At its best decision making calls for firmness in judgment. Decisions are influenced by facts, by evidence and by motives, by emotions and by the possible reactions of those affected by the decision, the opinions and judgment of others. In all of these elements the influence of the art of persuasion is seen.

Facts can be persuasive. Evidence of performance or salability can be persuasive. Motives have tremendous incentives and persuasive power. So do anticipated reactions and our emotions.

The art of persuasion becomes a potent factor in decision making when sales managers master this persuasive art.

Persuasive Power as an Antidote for Buck-Passing

A sales manager's memorandum of commendation circulated to his salesmen read as follows:

> Bill _____ , who covers the_____territory made an error in writing up an order for Mr. ____ , a customer of long standing. This could happen to any of us. Bill's customer was justifiably upset. He called the office to complain. We took it up with Bill at once. Without quibbling he accepted responsibility for the error. He also made a fast trip to see his customer and adjusted everything to the satisfaction of Mr. _____ .
>
> We commend Bill for acknowledging his error and for the effective manner in which he handled this problem.

The significant point in this case is that the sales manager focused attention on a salesman who accomplished much by not passing the buck. To admit error and accept what may follow requires courage and is worthy of commendation because buck-passing can kill morale in an organization.

An error in selling is seldom crucial. It becomes crucial, however, when the same error is repeated. An effective way to reduce error rate is to place a premium on perfection. Make more fuss over perfection than you do over an error.

Principle: Through persuasive action build confidence so strong in sales management that buck-passing becomes unpopular. "You can't escape the responsibility of tomorrow by evading it today," said Abraham Lincoln.

How to Feed Sales Power into Trouble Spots

Four types of knowledge are essential if sales management would effectively feed sales power into trouble spots. Consider these:

1. Knowledge of the capabilities of each member of your selling team and of each salesman's selling power.
2. Knowledge, including technical knowledge, of your product and its competitive place in the market and why it has attained this status.
3. Wide knowledge of how your product can be profitably used by the buyer and why and how your potential prospects can benefit from it.
4. Wide knowledge of your market, its peculiarities, its people, its needs, its wants, and its potentialities for contributing to your sales volume.

The sales director of a rapidly developing furniture production complex was asked: "What is the secret of your climbing sales volume?"

He replied: "Our sales manager holds the secret. I think it lies in his ability to eliminate trouble spots. He smothers trouble spots with sales power. He trains salesmen to heal a sore spot before it festers. Instead of dwelling too long on a complaint he lets go on the complainant with a strong sales pitch. He convinces complainants that he is all for them and for their welfare. He makes the complainant, not the complaint, the center of attention. By this method of close, man-to-man communication, our sales manager often winds up with a substantial order in addition to making the disgruntled customer happy."

This is one way in which the art of persuasion demonstrates its effectiveness in trouble-shooting. Case records prove that persuasion can be a productive tool for sales management and also for salesmen. The key to soothing trouble spots is to tackle problems persuasively, not to evade them.

Persuasive trouble-shooting is on a par with persuasive salesmanship. It is, in fact, selling. It is the art of influencing the other fellow to change his attitude from hostility to amiability. The most skillful trouble-shooters use a persuasive sales approach to calm troubled waters.

Principle: Stimulate salesmen to think their way through troubled areas. Teach them to substitute pleasant thoughts in the minds of complainants for unpleasant thoughts of things going haywire. By feeding sales power into trouble spots this persuasive power becomes a soothing application.

chapter 11

How to Knock Out Sales Hazards by Persuasive Action

Before we attack what we call sales hazards perhaps we should agree on what constitutes a hazard in selling.

A sales venture can become hazardous if it involves risk or loss. This could be the loss of an old customer. It could mean the risk of losing a substantial sale. It could be any risk involved in any sales venture. Sales hazards show up in the most unusual ways.

A sales hazard may be nothing more than uncertainty in the salesman's mind about closing a sale. As a general rule sales people are impressive as well as materialistic. Hazards can and usually do involve money. This should leave little doubt that we will encounter sales hazards in some form. A salesman may fumble in his presentation. This may leave the door wide open so a competitor can slip in and grab the business which the salesman had thought he had cinched.

It is difficult to separate hazards which affect salesmen from those which affect sales management. This should be made clear: What affects a salesman affects his sales manager and vice versa. Let us then examine a few familiar sales hazards which harass salesmen:

1. The possibility that the next prospect a salesman plans to meet will slam the door on him.

2. The possibility that a prospective account which a salesman has hoped to influence to buy from him turns out to be handled by a difficult, cantankerous buyer.
3. The discovery by a salesman that he is up against keen competition in an area where he had been led to believe he would have clear sailing.
4. The realization by a salesman that the majority of the accounts his sales manager has assigned to him are represented by buyers with whom the salesman has previously had personality clashes.

Let us now switch over to the hazards which sales managers may encounter. In the first place, every hazard we have identified as affecting salesmen is also a hazard in some way for sales managers. Until the hazard to the salesman is knocked out that obstacle to attaining maximum sales volume remains as a hazard to the sales manager, and, in fact, to the whole selling team.

So, in addition to the foregoing sales hazards, all of which are shared by salesmen and their sales managers, are other hazards directly related to sales management. Each salesman employed by a sales manager presents a risk to that sales manager. His success or his failure cannot get by without affecting the sales manager. There is nothing complicated or involved about this.

Most hazards in selling are primarily concerned with people. To a salesman a selling hazard represents a prospect. To a sales manager a sales hazard also represents people. It may represent a salesman's prospect, a salesman's account, or it may represent the salesman himself.

Objectives of sales managers and of salesmen are similar. A salesman's objective is to develop productive accounts. A sales manager's objective is proportionately larger. A sales manager's objective is the total of all of his salesmen's objectives plus his own dreams of their total increased sales volume. To attain his objective a sales manager must knock out sales hazards obstructing his salesmen. He must also teach his salesmen how to knock out those hazards which threaten to slow them down.

The only force which has been found to be generally effective against sales hazards is the art of persuasion in selling. It amounts to this: More people have to be influenced to buy more. This simplifies the problem. Sales managers who concentrate on developing persuasive selling power in their salesmen and who develop team spirit within their organizations usually come up with higher sales volume.

How, then, can this be accomplished? One answer: By sales management "selling" their salesmen on: (a) setting up individual production goals; (b) cooperating with management to achieve sales volume objectives set by management for the selling teams; (c) cooperating with other salesmen to minimize problems of the selling team as well as the problems of sales management.

All of this involves persuasive selling at its best. This is the persuasive way by which dynamic sales managers communicate with and inspire their selling teams to knock out sales hazards. This dynamic sales force is used by dynamic sales managers to restrain sales hazards of every kind. It contains the simple principles of the persuasive art. It can lift salesmen out of mediocrity and raise them up to high production. When this is achieved it becomes the moment of triumph for sales management against sales hazards.

Persuasive Ways to Combat "Ghosts" That Kill Sales

Don't be misled. In reality there *are* ghosts and they do intrude on the domain of sales managers. These ghosts drain off productive energy from salesmen. They sabotage sales managers' plans for sales expansion. However, there is one bright spot in this picture: *Sales management has found a way to combat these sales-killing ghosts.*

Four of the most insidious ghosts which prey on salesmen and sales managers are the following.

Ghost No. 1—Worry

This ghost is a sadist. It tortures its victims. It creates mental images of impending disaster, but it seldom produces a real disaster. Nevertheless, Ghost No. 1 is a qualified sales killer.

Ghost No. 2—Fear

This ghost is dedicated to the proposition that streaks of cowardice exist in every salesman and in every sales manager. It weakens courage. It numbs originality. It neutralizes creative talent. It destroys initiative. Ghost No. 2 is a rival of Ghost No. 1 as a sales-killer.

Ghost No. 3—Indecision

This ghost is an aggressive foe of positive, constructive salesmanship and sales management. This ghost sets up phantom-like obstacles to keep vacillating sales managers off balance. Then this ghost whispers to them: "Don't you dare make a firm decision." Ghost No. 3 contributes heavily to sales casualties.

Ghost No. 4—Indifference

This is a negative ghost—a head-shaker. It creates doubt. It down-grades any well-planned objective of sales management. It steals the pep of salesmen and sales executives alike. It fogs their vision. It's a treacherous ghost, a troublemaker for sales managers. It preys on the whole selling team. Once under way, Ghost No. 4 becomes a whiz at killing sales.

There you have the ghost lineup. You should know and understand this quartet of sales saboteurs. Only then can you combat them. Four tested methods are suggested for knocking out these sales-killing ghosts:

Target No. 1—the Ghost of Worry

The divisional sales manager for a management consulting firm said: "I tried to worry myself to success. I didn't make it. I discovered that one day of worry took more out of me than a week of hard work. So I kicked the fretting habit and converted that energy into better direction of my salesmen. In this way I hit pay dirt. My whole sales team profited when I got the worry monkey off my back."

The key to combating the worry habit is this: Face up to your problem. Do what must be done to solve it. In this way you clear the decks for the next problem. Winston Churchill proved that he was a persuasive salesman. He "sold" the British people on his formula for defeating the Nazis. He said this about worry: "In my life I have worried about a lot of things, most of which never happened."

Several giants in industry have had to conquer the ghost of worry. A sales manager's responsibility includes the training of men to become worry-free. But, this does not anticipate that he should worry about his duties. To become a dynamic sales manager one rises above the sales-killing ghost of worry. It is when a sales manager tears himself away from this ghost that he develops sales in volume through the art of persuasion.

Target No. 2—The Ghost of Fear

"To nourish fear is fatal to selling," said the sales manager of a large automobile distributorship. "The salesman who is fearful in the presence of a prospect is in bad shape. Yet I have seen fearful salesmen rise above this handicap and become top producers." They conquered fear by recognizing that to pamper fear is to become intimate with a ghost. When this nation was stricken with fear in a great depression Franklin D. Roosevelt told the people there was nothing to fear but fear itself.

Target No. 3—The Ghost of Indecision

Said one industrialist: "Indecision is a habit. You can break that habit by making one courageous decision: That you will promptly view the bare bones of the worst problem that now faces you and that you will stare at those bones until you make up your mind what you must do to solve that problem. Then act on your decision. That's the whole secret of conquering indecision."

Sales managers who succeed in teaching salesmen to be decisive take the first step toward combating indecision in themselves. In doing that they witness the sales-killing influence of indecision. They also gain courage themselves to free themselves of this ghost which they can do through the art of persuasion in sales management.

Target No. 4—The Ghost of Indifference

Indifference is the sin of sins in sales management. To combat indifference sales managers become sensitive to the problems of each salesman on the selling teams. They take a positive, constructive, worry-free look at those problems because those problems affect their total sales volume. Too often indifference is an escape device. It can become a habitual method of dodging an unpleasant or burdensome duty. Indifference is a state of mind. If permitted to go on unchallenged indifference has a tendency to become tyrannical in its effect. It may destroy self-confidence. It cuts into efficiency. It cools the desire of the sales team to excell in performance. This sales-killing ghost has been known to throw in the towel when the power of the art of persuasion in sales management begins punching.

The four sales-killing ghosts are all related to personalities—the worrier, the fearful type, the indecisive sales executive, the indifferent salesman and his indifferent sales manager. All of these victims of sales-killing ghosts are vulnerable to power in the art of persuasion. Mastery of this art is identified with dynamic sales management. Self-confident sales managers exert persuasive influence on their selling teams and thereby push up sales volume. These sales managers are positive personalities. They are not the worriers, the fearful ones, or the indecisive ones, or the indifferent personalities. Sales-killing ghosts just do not survive in a climate dominated by persuasive salesmen and persuasive sales managers.

How to Apply Patient, Persistent, Persuasive Pressure

We now add a fourth element to the "Three P" formula which was previously introduced. We add "Persistence" and come up with a "Four P" formula for sales management purposes—Patience, Perception, Persistence, and Persuasion.

Salesmen apply persuasive pressure on prospects to influence them to buy. Sales managers apply patient, persistent pressure on salesmen to persuade them to become more persuasive and consequently to sell more.

How does our "Four P" formula stack up as a factor in applying pressure on those who sell? Let us examine this formula:

Patience—Rousseau, one of the most influential thinkers of his age, left this thought for us: "Patience is bitter, but its fruit sweet." Sales management may find encouragement in that observation.

Perception—The perceptive sales manager has insight into problems which affect his selling team. He sees the need for pressure and the areas where pressure should be applied. He sees things from the salesman's point of view. He understands. As Emerson said: "He is a new man with new perceptions."

Persistence—Calvin Coolidge told us that "nothing in the world can take the place of persistence." This may be debatable but sales records provide evidence that persistence is the great virtue of dynamic sales managers.

Persuasion—In exercising patience, with perception, and also in persistence, we are concerned with persuasive power. As a sales manager you strive for tangible results. The art of persuasion gives this to you. The key to power in the art of persuasion is cooperation. Persuasive sales managers get united action out of salesmen by the spirit of "Come on, gang, let's put it over." The cooperative way develops producing sales teams.

An indirect method of applying pressure on his selling team was used by one sales manager with favorable results. He ran "Salesmen Wanted" ads in the newspaper. In those ads he listed qualifications for applicants. His own men read those ads. He had expected that they would. The salesmen talked among themselves about those ads. Their conversation was in this vein: "The boss is looking for guys who show a lot of zip. I wonder how I measure up. Man, we'd better get with it."

Another sales manager applies "patient pressure" on his salesmen by increasing his requirements on those who demonstrate that they are in the business to succeed. He feeds their spirit by assuring them that he believes they can produce more sales than they are doing.

Most dynamic sales managers are perceptive and persistent men. They step up sales volume by persistent, persuasive pressure. They produce sales volume through the art of persuasion. They provide incentives for their selling teams. They encourage salesmen by recognizing and rewarding exceptional accomplishments.

Five Ways to Release the Full Sales Energy of Your Staff

Bottled up in each salesman on your staff is more productive energy than he expends in active selling. This has been established by various studies. Bottled up in every selling team is an untapped reservoir of sales energy. This presents a constant challenge to sales managers to *uncork that energy,* to get it to flow out in a persuasive flood and to create greater and more profitable sales volume.

This untapped energy is held back by non-selling forces which steal a salesman's time. This is, or should be, a major concern to sales management. This waste can be cut down by more constructive planning and through the art of persuasion.

Five ways have been suggested for releasing the full sales energy of your staff. The following methods have been tried with productive results:

1. Build confidence in sales management by minimizing time-consuming requirements. Reevaluate administrative requirements made on salesmen eliminating all non-essentials. Strive to avoid worry and emotional storms which burn up fuel which can better be used to keep the selling machine on the road. "Sell" all requirements and every idea which you present to your salesmen. Convince them that what you are asking is in their best interest. This is persuasion at work to release maximum energy for the selling process.

2. Stimulate the "up and at 'em" attitude in your sales team by downgrading mishaps. Encourage the man who stumbles to regain his footing. Counteract the depressing effect of a blunder by playing up a noteworthy accomplishment. This is how dynamic sales managers cash in on the art of persuasion.

3. Keep the door ajar. Let your salesmen be heard. Convince them that you believe they are the backbone of your operation. Take a back seat at times. Let a salesman have the floor. What he says may have persuasive power. Let the art of persuasion work its magic in that way.

4. Let there be light! Keep salesmen informed. They work with greater purpose in the light than in darkness. Distrust in sales management is fostered by darkness. Keep salesmen posted on additions to the line, on price changes, and, of course, on policy changes. Full information fed to

the selling team tends to suppress rumors which create misunderstanding. This is the art of persuasion in sales management. It strengthens team spirit.

5. Dynamic sales managers are tough-minded listeners. As Edgar Dale, the educator, once said:'"The tough-minded listener . . . is neither a slave to unrelated facts nor at the mercy of sweeping generalities." Listen to your salesmen. When they turn to you in confidence you reap the rich harvest of the art of persuasion in sales management. In such moments you can uncork bottled up sales energy in members of your staff. Wilson Mizner, the humorist, saw persuasive value in listening. He said: "A good listener is not only popular, but after a while he knows something."

Persuasive Devices for Increasing Production

In the jargon of sales managers and salesmen production means sales. It means correct orders. It means orders that are O.K.'d by buyers, approved by credit managers, and certified for shipment. The goal of dynamic sales managers is to accelerate the production of such orders. Sales managers who attain that objective use a variety of persuasive devices. Among the devices which have proved their effectiveness in producing sales volume are these:

1. System
2. Objectives
3. Purpose
4. Coordination
5. Unity

Sales management has found that a well-defined "M.O." can be a persuasive device in developing sales. "M.O." means "method of operation." In sales management the M.O. covers a wide field.

—It includes rules to regulate routine procedures.

—It clarifies house policies.

—It sets forth the limits of a salesman's authority and responsibility.

—It specifies channels to follow for orderly communication between salesmen and executives.

—It identifies executive responsibilities.

—It is the system which makes all of the foregoing and more possible. Experience has proved that when the system is understood all the way from sales management to the end of the selling team that production goes up and things work smoothly. There are persuasive qualities in an orderly house. *System* is the key to orderliness.

Clearly defined objectives stimulate sales production. Salesmen who know where they are going and what their talents are become higher producers. Higher production has a way of falling into line when sales managers clearly define the all-over objectives of a sales campaign.

Established objectives stimulate thinking. While the entire sales team may understand what the sales team is expected to accomplish, each salesman, being a creative thinker, will have his own persuasive method for "doing his thing." The combination of clearly defined objectives of sales managers and the creative thinking of individual salesmen in a unified team provide impressive persuasive power.

But, even objectives must have a *purpose.* That purpose should be made clear to salesmen. This will persuade them to throw their full persuasive power into the action. A successful sales director of a chain automobile distributorship put it this way to his selling team: "We have gone into our sales plan thoroughly. We believe we have the bugs out. We now have a definite purpose in what we are attempting to do and how we propose to do it." He then detailed his plan. He got enthusiastic response from his salesmen. The result: Sales went up all along the line. Why? Because every man knew the plan and how he fit into it. It was "sold" to them through the art of persuasion in sales management.

The structure of a new home aroused the admiration of a construction engineer. His friend, a seasoned real estate sales manager, asked him: "Will it sell?" The dismayed engineer replied: "I wouldn't know. Why?" His sales-minded friend replied: "Your objective was to build a fine home in which you have pride. That's great, but my first interest is: Will it sell?"

When a sales manager succeeds in establishing a workable system and he sets forth appealing and sound objectives, and then outlines his purpose for doing this he is prepared to move into the next phase of increasing sales production—*coordination.* This is the key link in the chain. When every man on his selling team is tied into that chain by a system of coordination that sales manager has established one more persuasive device for increasing production. Coordination simply means that everybody is involved. It means that everybody gets the word, even on the smallest detail as well as the larger details affecting the system.

Principle: Coordinate for team work and for maximum persuasive selling power.

A sales manager has achieved *unity* in his selling team when (a) all the persuasive devices he may have set in motion are securely hooked together in a coordinated chain; and (b) when all objectives and purposes he has outlined are clearly understood and accepted by the selling team.

Unity is the key device for increasing sales production through the art of persuasion in sales management.

Why Sales Success Should Be Pulled Apart

Success, and its opposite, *failure,* have certain persuasive qualities. Sales management and salesmen can profit by both experiences.

The dynamic sales manager becomes concerned with two developments affecting his business: (1) successfully wrapping up a difficult sale; (2) losing a desirable sale. Both of these developments reflect on him. His sales training program and his leadership are under a cloud when a desirable sale is lost. In the first instance he sees the fruit of his training and his leadership. In the second instance an imaginative sales manager can see new possibilities for the art of persuasion to develop sales volume on the ruins of the sales effort that failed. To attain this sales building objective he critically examines the failure. He probes for some concealed lesson in salesmanship which can make this one failure a profitable development.

In the case of a successful sale a sales manager can ask: Why did it turn out so well? How could it have been made more productive? Such curiosity can persuade him to turn on the light so he can peer into dark areas of salesmanship. He searches for the *how* and the *why* in *successes* as well as in *failures.* With his curiosity deepening the sales manager persists in trying to find constructive answers to questions such as these:

The Lost Sale: How did it happen? Why did it happen? Was it due to an error in judgment? Did the salesman ignore instructions? Did he encounter unforeseen obstacles? How did he react to these obstacles? Was he weak in persuasion? What finally influenced the prospective buyer to refuse to buy? What reason did he give for not buying? How could the salesman have avoided a flat turn-down? How can he reapproach this prospect persuasively?

The In-the-Bag Sale: How was this difficult sale landed? What persuasive power did the salesman release to land this sale? How did the salesman turn on this power? What step-by-step process did he follow in leading the prospect from the point of interest to a favorable decision? How did the salesman maintain persuasive interest and selling pressure? What resistance did he encounter? How did he react to this resistance? What was the most persuasive factor in the successful conclusion of this sale?

Most of us are adept at pulling failures apart. We pick at the lost sale until the bare skeleton of the case is fully exposed to view. At times we overlook the fact that the failure we have been plucking apart may contain an idea that can be converted into a profitable sale by simply combining that idea with persuasive power. The perceptive sales manager sees such favorable possibilities even in lost sales.

Success deserves the most critical examination of all developments in selling. By pulling apart each success with the same vigor displayed in tearing into failures a sales manager can determine, for the benefit of the whole selling team, *how* the sale was made and *how* it could possibly have been more profitable. To do this constructively dynamic sales managers rely heavily on the art of persuasion. They persuade their selling teams to: (a) accept failure as a challenge and a tonic; (b) recognize that success in one sale is a vitalizing experience which can motivate salesmen to aspire to greater production. It can also give them strength to endure and profit by possible reverses in the future. This is the constructive, persuasive objective of dynamic sales managers in pulling apart sales successes.

Persuasive Ways to Uncover Causes of Lost Sales

Sales managers hear a variety of reasons why salesmen wind up a day with a zero on the sales chart. Some of these tales pique the curiosity of sales managers. Consider these four categories in which sales are frequently lost.

The Projected "Sure Thing" Sale Which Turns Sour on the Salesman

Over-confidence is a common cause for losing sales. One understanding sales manager sat down with one of his salesmen who had lost a "sure thing" sale. This salesman had banked on that order. Losing it was a double shock to him. It stung his pride. It shook up his bank account. Anticipating the sale he had spent unwisely. But, through the art of persuasion his understanding sales manager restored that salesman's self-confidence when he discovered the real reason why the salesman lost the sale. The reason: Over-confidence. The salesman had become less persuasive. Cocksure of landing the sale he took it easy. His prospect also became relaxed—so relaxed that he decided there was no urgency and took the easy way out. He made no decision, except that he would wait awhile.

The Declining Ratio of Sales to the Number of Calls Made

A tested, effective way of uncovering this cause of lost sales is this: Persuasively but persistently squeeze out the facts. Discuss each call individually with the salesman. Keep this discussion on an informal basis—informality has a certain persuasive quality. Slowly the facts come out. Too many of those calls had degenerated into social calls instead of selling calls. True, friends had been cultivated on these calls, but sales had not.

The Low Ratio of Sales Closed on Assigned Calls

Person-to-person dialogue with salesmen on such calls often reveals that the salesmen were not at their best on these assigned calls. Behind this there usually is a reason, too. In one such case the salesman resented being told where to prospect for business. He saw no importance in his assignment. The importance of the call had not been built up for him. This was a strike against sales management. But his sales manager, recognizing where the problem began turned on his persuasive art and inspired this salesman to go after those prospects for the sake of the team record. This he did, and he scored high in sales.

The Declining Number of New Accounts Opened

This is the simplest of all categories to penetrate in searching for reasons why sales are dropping. Perceptive sales management soon detects what is wrong. As one sales manager defined it: "Relaxed selling writes less and less new business. A salesman who has had a 'comfortable' group of accounts over several years may drift into a relaxed pace. He makes fewer and fewer calls on new prospects. He is a good salesman but he is content to sacrifice the thrill of writing new business." Another well-seasoned sales executive had this prescription for restoring such salesmen to high production: "It's a rare salesman," he said, "who can't be bounced out of his self-imposed contentment by appealing to his self-interest."

The art of persuasion appears in various disguises. Yet, this art in sales management uncovers cases of lost sales every working day. It discloses weaknesses, reveals strength, revives interest, awakens purpose, and motivates salesmen to "reach for the skies" in sales production.

chapter 12

How to Profitably
Manage the Sex
Issue in Selling

Sex in sales management? It's as real as your overdraft in the bank. In selling you are involved in the sex problem. As a sales manager you have little hope of avoiding it. Your success may even depend upon how "hep" you are on sex in business. Let's take a look at selling from a sex angle.

What about your most substantial customers? Isn't there somewhere in their organizations the influence of a woman, or of women, on what they buy? Don't they have wives, and daughters, and secretaries? Don't you suppose these attractive, intelligent, persistent feminine persons influence those who make the final decisions in buying? And, then, haven't you had the experience of discovering that one of your choice accounts was owned by a woman? You can bet your brief case that she had something to say about buying. This affected you as a sales manager. No doubt your best salesmen are reasonably well oriented on the sex angle in selling. They buy candy and flowers and things such as that for secretaries who guard doors to the offices of desirable prospects. Those little acts of friendly bribery inject a sex angle into your business. The more thought you give to it the more involved you become in the fascinating issue of sex in selling.

Now let's consider your competitor in that area where you have been striving to get reasonable sales volume. What happened when you found out that the sales manager of that aggressive outfit was a woman? You probably inquired into the reasons why a female competitor had so impressively slipped into your business life. You may have found out that she came up to her position as sales manager the hard way. She had more than sex appeal to hold down that job. She knew the in's and out's about selling. She also knew that in order to beat you and other competing sales managers she would have to be up front in selling know-how. She knew that when she accepted the sales manager's job that male salesmen, her own and those on competitive selling teams, would be sizing her up. She was quite sure that those men would be selfish in their appraisal of her—that they would be looking for executive ability and selling "savvy," and not primarily for curves. She understood, or she soon would understand, that she would have to learn more about men. She became sure that she would have to find out what, besides sex appeal, would "turn on" her salesmen and motivate them to become better salesmen.

The stern reality of the sex issue in selling from the sales manager's angle is this: Either through trial and error, prior knowledge, or by insight into the female mind the male sales manager must learn precisely the same things about women in selling that he must learn about the salesmen on his selling team. In this the sales manager faces four challenging sex issues:

—Sex Problem No. 1: To devise ways to motivate women to sell.
—Sex Problem No. 2: To inspire women to become creative sales people.
—Sex Problem No. 3: To provide leadership of such quality that even the opposite sex will say: "I'll buy that."
—Sex Problem No. 4: To profitably manage the sex issue in selling.

The latter may be the toughest problem of all. But, there is this encouragement: People, male and female, respond to stimulation which appeals to their self-interest. One dynamic sales manager who has several women on his field selling team said the secret of his success in handling the sex issue was "keeping sex out of the business. They are all sales people," he said. "I draw no sex line."

What was once considered to be a man's world in business has been modified. Women have been demonstrating that they have more than sex appeal on which to capitalize. Women are challenging men in the executive field, not on a sex basis, but on a performance basis. This is a formidable challenge by formidable rivals in sales management. The male attitude of accepting this challenge is indicative of change. For instance a journalistic fraternity which has kept its doors closed to women for 60 years has opened their doors and admitted the girls to membership.

Gallantry may be dead but self-interest is very much alive even when the sex issue enters the business or professional arena.

The observation of Esther Peterson, once Secretary of Labor, is illuminating. She simplifies the problem. "If we want women to work we must face the fact that men and women are different," she said. On this brief statement hangs the secret by which sales management can profitably manage the sex issue in selling.

Introducing Mr. Salesman to His Formidable Rival

Women have become career-minded. They have become achievement-minded. In brief, women have entered the market place recognizing all that it entails. This can put vitality into selling. It pits female rivals against the best salesmen on selling teams. These formidable rivals are those once referred to as of "the weaker sex." They are the "ladies" of yesterday. They are those who once tested the chivalry of men.

In the business arena women already have demonstrated that they have qualifications for achievement in selling:

1. Talent—Women have intelligence, persuasiveness, insight, intuition and persistence.
2. Sex Appeal—This is an endowment of nature, glorified by all other talents of women.

There is no rule in commerce which states that women have no right to aspire to greatness in the field of selling. Today two pay checks in the family have become accepted routine. Married women have decided to compete with men on men's terms. With this has come a new concept of the capabilities and the persuasive power of women. The result is rivalry between men and women in the market place.

The woman sitting in a waiting room next to your highest rated salesman also wants to get in to see your most preferred customer. She may be the wife of your salesman's best friend in his favorite golf club. That closeness, however, takes a back seat at this moment. He and that woman are there to sell to the prospective buyer behind the closed door. Both intend to do so. This is a case of man vs. woman rivalry. The dual pay check trend in family life has greater significance. This affects the overall economy. This gets right down to the case of sales management talent. This interest is broader than the individual objectives of one salesman and his female rival. The trend of two pay checks in each family recognizes woman's place in the economic picture. In a material sense the sex issue is definitely involved here. The earning power and the buying power of women go far beyond the wildest dreams of yesterday's brides.

Alert sales managers are aware of this expanding market. In reality this accounts for the exploitation of feminine selling talent by dynamic sales managers.

In the rough and tumble game of selling as it is played in the market place the average female is not inhibited by shyness. She has gone into selling with her sights set high, her eyes wide open, her courage and confidence at top level. She has studied. She has prepared for this venture. And, now that she has kicked open the door to opportunity for personal gain for herself in the market place she refuses to stand still. We find women in direct selling, in retail selling, in the field representing some of our greater industries. We find them selling real estate, insurance, and automobiles. These feminine rivals of salesmen are versatile sales people in fields once largely dominated by men.

In addition to married women we also have another feminine rival of men in selling. This one also has sex appeal and she has selling talent. She is young. She thinks she has squared away her objectives and has settled on selling as a career. She intends to squeeze out of selling all that it will yield. She is in this game to win, just as she has seen her mother and other mature women succeed. She finds no reason why she should sit on her hands and allow the married women to win the big stakes. She firmly believes that she is capable of producing sales. As a sales manager you are inclined to agree with her. This is self-interest on your part. You have an eye on greater sales volume and you can see how this young woman, fired up with enthusiasm, can get some of that sales volume for you. There is one catch, however, to such objectives of an ambitious single girl turned saleswoman. Behind her materialistic objectives lurks the shadow of another phase in self-interest. At heart she may really be mate-hunting. Here we have the sex issue again. Many sales managers have experienced romance snatching promising saleswomen from their selling teams. Nevertheless, when a woman, single or married, hits the jackpot in selling she gains a new independence in life. A new sense of security takes possession of her. It is on this spirit that sales managers can capitalize. Such women are motivated to continue climbing, to sell more and more. They dare to enter more competitive fields. They dare to study and venture into technical fields of selling. Noting this, sales managers with an eye on progress smile, because such rivalry is bound to awaken male members on their selling teams to "reach for the skies" in selling.

John Ruskin, who became known for his rebellion against the materialistic standards of Victorian England, had this to say about sex superiority:

"We are foolish, and without excuse foolish, in speaking of the superiority of one sex to the other, as if they could be compared in similar things! Each has what the other has not; each completes the other; they are in nothing alike; and the happiness and perfection of both depend on each asking and receiving from the other what the other only can give."

Sales managers might profit by pondering Ruskin's viewpoint when they become perplexed with the problems of management of the sex issue in selling and also when they introduce Mr. Salesman to a formidable rival with sex appeal.

None of this, of course, excludes sex as a potent force in selling.

Five Keys to Capitalizing on Sex in Selling

There is now little question about women being formidable competitors of men in selling. Records prove this to be true. But, the sales manager's problem goes beyond the ability to sell. It involves the "how" of capitalizing on feminine ability to produce sales in profitable volume. Assuming then that a male sales manager has a woman, or a number of women, on his selling team, at once he is confronted with this challenge: *"How can I capitalize on the persuasive power in those women to produce sales for me?"*

Here are five keys for male sales managers with which they can open that hope chest and get at its riches:

1. Capitalize on the persuasive feminine viewpoint to improve planning for increasing sales volume.
2. Capitalize on the persuasive feminine viewpoint to achieve unity of purpose in the selling team for increasing sales volume.
3. Capitalize on female responsiveness to sales incentives to develop greater sales volume.
4. Capitalize on those persuasive qualities with which women are endowed to break down sales resistance.
5. Capitalize on dual persuasive power and dual viewpoints for the benefit of both men and women on the selling team.

Key No. 1—The all-male viewpoint in a sales plan may lack that delicate, persuasive touch to which both women and men respond. Sales managers might well invite women on their sales staffs to appraise their selling plans. Women so invited should have demonstrated leadership qualities. They could be asked to criticize selling plans and to suggest improvements. Such women have been known to amaze their sales managers by their depth of perception.

Key No. 2—That same persuasive power, that same discernment which proved profitable to you for improving your selling plan is also available to you in unifying your selling team. Get the woman's viewpoint on how women and men can pull together to develop greater sales volume. The art of persuasion is involved here. It can reveal the power of a woman to do, or to persuade others to achieve, what she wants to accomplish.

Key No. 3—Sales incentives are a favorite tool of sales managers. They are good, bad, or indifferent to the extent that they produce sales in volume. On sales incentives the woman's viewpoint may be shocking to you. It may also be beneficial. What you, Mr. Sales Manager, may think will appeal persuasively to women on your selling team may fall flat. However, the discerning woman whom you have called in to advise you may immediately detect the weakness in your incentive plan. Capitalize on her intuition and on her viewpoint and on her persuasive power.

Key No. 4—That tough prospect who has defied your efforts to draw him into your customer net may turn out to be easy prey for one of your experienced saleswomen. It's a blow to male ego, of course, to have a woman go into the den of such a prospect and come out with a substantial order in her brief case. Nevertheless this has happened. So, this tip for sales managers is valid: Never underestimate the persuasive power of a woman, even with an obstinate prospect.

Key No. 5—The man and wife team is a gambler's choice. You may profit by it on your selling team. It has the advantage of providing dual viewpoint in sales volume development. Here the friendly rivalry of man vs. woman receives close concentration to develop sales. This is simply another way of capitalizing on the feminine viewpoint in selling. With both men and women on your selling team you have the ego of the male and the female pitted against each other. Sales often climb with this sort of competitive spirit.

Much of the foregoing has been aimed at male sales managers. What, then, does the female sales manager do to profitably manage the sex issue in selling? The answer is quite simple: *Get the male viewpoint and capitalize on it.* By reversing the viewpoint in the five keys to capitalizing on sex in selling, the female sales manager makes those keys applicable to her.

Women in selling have some advantages which men generally recognize are beyond their competitive power. *Women have more sex appeal than men.* Women also have a favored position. At least men believe that they do. Men, for instance, believe that the cantankerous buyer won't go all out and blow his top in the presence of a petite saleswoman. Women have the notion that such a woman is loaded with sex appeal which is persuasive enough to wrap up a sale from obstinate buyers. Of course men believe they are right. In time, however, they learn that it takes more than that to secure and keep business.

Some men on your selling team may also have the notion that women buyers will be push-overs for them. They are so self-confident about their own sex appeal that they believe that militant female buyers will wilt before them. Usually the truth will out. Such over-confident men eventually learn that they overlooked a woman's greatest asset. They forgot about feminine intuition. If any of your salesmen haven't been up against a woman's intuition, their moment of enlightenment will be a great day for you and for those salesmen. Women in business are usually sharp. They see through the guy who assumes that women will swoon when he walks in. As Victor Hugo put it: "Men have sight, but women have insight."

Dynamic male sales managers capitalize on the insight of women.

Dynamic female sales managers capitalize on understanding the male viewpoint.

It's the persuasive thing to do in profitably managing the sex issue in selling.

Tips for Motivating Women to Sell More

Can you imagine anything but more money that will motivate women to put more zest into their sales efforts?

Isn't a woman's objective in selling the same as a man's objectives?

Judging from figures released by the U. S. Department of Labor it would seem that someone along the line slipped in motivating women to sell more. These figures indicate that the average earnings of women in sales falls below the average earnings of men. This presents a challenge to sales management to provide more motivation for women in sales.

I recall a rural area in which deaths had left a number of penniless widows because farmer-husbands had died without insurance coverage. Here was high motivation for a woman in life insurance sales. Her male associates discouraged her. "We've worked that territory," they said. "You're wasting time with those farmers." But she replied: "I believe you're wrong. I have death and sex appeal going for me in a big way." And, she went after business.

This woman saw a tragic need for what she had to sell and this motivated her. In turn she motivated unwidowed women in that area to motivate their husbands to buy insurance. This ran up high sales volume for that highly motivated woman.

How can sales managers in other lines motivate their women in sales to sell more? Sales records provide tips such as these:

Encourage women in sales to capitalize on the sex angle. The self-motivated woman in life insurance sales did just that. She persuaded men to provide protection for their wives against penniless widowhood. This was a cold, practical approach to the sex angle in selling. She pitted the self-interest of wives against indecisive husbands. She made her sales appeal direct and persuasive to both husbands and wives. She got the business because she was highly motivated.

Challenge women on your selling team to out-do the men. An area sales manager for a large national advertising art calendar house threw down a challenge of that sort to the only woman he had on his selling team. On the opening day of the new line she took off with samples of only one exclusive subject. This art subject had high local appeal in her territory. Her objective: To sell this advertising calendar on an exclusive basis to one house in each community capable of buying in quantity. Using tried and tested sales pitches of pride, prestige, and business-building advertising power she wrote business in volume. She capitalized on the sex issue, too. When men wavered she got their women employees worked up about her idea. Out of this she got sales. When one austere woman who ran the biggest business in a small town shied away from the calendar idea, this sales woman capitalized on her alertness. She had heard the assistant manager, a handsome, middle-aged man, speak gently to the female boss of the establishment and call her by her first name. She turned her persuasive power on this man. He influenced the female executive to seize the opportunity for exclusive promotion in the community. This closed the sale.

Set up a target for women in sales. Give them something to shoot at. Make it attractive. Motivate them to succeed. Show them what other women in sales are achieving and show them how to do better.

Women can sell as well as buy. To sell more they require motivation just as men require motivation. In the retail market women are among the big buyers. They are suspected of controlling the purse strings of families of the nation. These women pride themselves on being keen judges of merchandise. They believe they can judge values. They also believe they are sharp in judging character. With all this in their favor they do have a potential in salesmanship. All this presents a challenge to sales management. It is up to them to provide motivation for women on their selling teams to persuade these women to buy what they have to sell.

Ego plays a strong part in motivation. Women in sales want to enjoy the personal satisfaction of being top producers on the selling team. Motivate them to "reach for the skies in selling."

Motivation is the energy source which propels desire into productive action. Motivation is the basic success principle for effective management of the sex issue in selling. Motivation is based on the art of persuasion, a highly productive art for sales managers to master.

How Women Boost Sales by Persuasion

Women who enter selling come in three classifications:

1. *The Daring Type*—They accept selling as a challenge. They crave new opportunities to grapple with difficult buyers, male and female.
2. *The Adventurous Type*—Male competition fascinates these women. They are out to prove they can outsell the men, and they often do.
3. *The Exploring Type*—These women have a double objective: (a) to make money; (b) to attract desirable men. Once Cupid gets in his sales pitch, selling loses part of its glamour.

One sales manager with extensive experience said: "Most of us in sales management have a few explorers on our staffs. Usually they are attractive, intelligent, and ambitious. We hire them on the basis of these qualifications plus the gamble that they will become sales producers. When I find out that I have been outsold by Dan Cupid I scratch that gal off my list and renew my search for a dedicated saleswoman who will develop volume for me."

Sex seldom becomes a factor with the daring type woman in sales. Her sights are set on getting business. It is a personal business with her. She may be a striking beauty but she does not flaunt her femininity. She is persistent, courteous, pleasant, and very persuasive. Her sales presentations have one objective: To sell! She capitalizes on her femininity by capturing attention, holding on to that attention, and by persuasive selling. She makes a cold, calculated, dollar-sign sales pitch trimmed with the warmth of feminine persuasiveness. This usually wraps up a sale whether the buyer is male or female.

The adventurous type woman in sales has all the qualities of the daring type plus relentless competitive spirit. She is friendly but challenging. She is an asset to the sales staff. She keeps male sales people on their toes. She is resourceful; a builder of sales who thrives on topping sales records of the men.

Women in sales often rate high in contacts with women buyers. For the daring and adventurous type saleswomen they work as hard to get business from women buyers as from male buyers. The adventurous type female is reluctant to admit that any man on the sales team can outsell her in confrontation with a female prospect. These dynamic saleswomen demonstrate that sales volume is built on persuasive sales power rather than on sex appeal.

A woman who built sales volume in newspaper advertising said the secret of success in her business is: (a) "Be on the level. When people believe in you enough to call on you for advice you're in; (b) Talk about profits, about values, and about personal benefits. I never talk about the cost of advertising. I talk about an investment and how well it pays off."

A widow who revived the failing bakery business which her husband left said: "Straight-from-the-shoulder selling put this business back on its feet. I built volume in this way. I train our men and women in sales to go after business in the same way. I tell the women I employ for sales that any attempt by them to get business just because they are attractive creatures will cheapen them in the eyes of buyers and will cheapen this business. I will have none of that."

This persuasive saleswoman succeeded in two ways: (1) She developed sales volume; (2) she developed productive salesmen and saleswomen, all through the art of persuasion coupled with feminine persistence and determination.

What Men Can Learn from the Techniques of Women in Leadership and Selling

By recognizing a sales problem we can more clearly evaluate the techniques of women in solving it. Consider these five sales-producing points with feminine connections:

1. Feminine persuasiveness and persistence presents a formidable attack on the most stubborn sales resistance. (Salesmen and sales executives take note.)
2. Feminine ability to turn personal charm on and off at will is an asset in winning a point or closing a sale. (Salesmen and male sales managers with personal charm take note.)
3. Feminine determination to surmount obstacles and to press on toward an objective has a record of cracking sales resistance. (Salesmen and male sales managers take note.)
4. Feminine ability to pit a woman's charm against the charm of a male prospect and retain persuasive mastery of the sales interview is an accomplishment which results in sales. (Salesmen and male sales managers take note.)
5. Feminine ability to disregard the fact that both sexes are involved in her effort to capture a desirable slice of available business erases the sex problem as such. It places the selling process on a solid, dollar-paying basis. (Salesmen and male sales managers take note and profit by emulating this feminine quality.)

Take it from Earl Nightingale, a business executive, it requires considerable depth of understanding for a male sales manager to acquire knowledge about leadership or about salesmanship by observing how women apply their skills in selling. The problem, according to Mr. Nightingale, is this:

"Not being able to understand women wouldn't be so bad if they didn't understand men. Actually the so-called weaker sex is the stronger sex because of the weakness of the stronger sex for the weaker sex."

Perhaps men can learn about outselling feminine competitors by observing how women go about selling. Notice the fury, the determination in a woman's eyes when she is denied something she eagerly wants. Competition arouses her fighting spirit. She drives harder to get business if competition tries to deny her those sales which she wants.

Men, too, can profit by becoming less content to let sales opportunities by-pass them. By nature women are more inquisitive than men. They enjoy "exploring." In their desire to reach out and see, women often uncover rich sales possibilities. At times they display uncanny ability to sense when the sales winds are favorable to them. (Salesmen and male sales managers take note and profit by more depth in sales exploration.)

Helen Wills, the tennis star, was known as "Little Poker Face." She had intense competitive drive. It was this drive, plus skill, which propelled her up to be crowned a champion. Men in selling can profit by developing similar desire to set up sales records. By developing more thrust in leadership sales managers have been known to lead selling teams into the championship class.

A woman who came up from the production and marketing side of an advertising agency attained her objective to own and operate her own agency. She had a husband and she had children. From them she drew inspiration. "My most profitable sales product," she once said, "is an idea. I get new ideas from my family. My kids and my husband see and hear TV commercials. They spot the good ones and the phony ones. Believe me, they tell me about them. I give their ideas a lot of serious thought. Their ideas may mean business for me. The kid market, for instance, is a big one. I can profit by an idea that ties in with selling to kids. Those who work for me can also profit by such ideas. My clients can also profit."

This woman is a formidable competitor of salesmen and male sales promotion executives in her field.

How to profitably manage the sex issue in selling is a challenge to sales executives. The stakes are high. The art of persuasion plays a dominant part in meeting that challenge. This art is deeply involved in the male-female relationship in selling. Dynamic sales managers capitalize on persuasive power.

chapter 13

How to Make Your
Sales Conferences
More Persuasive

The conference hour had arrived. Salesmen pushed away from their desks and lumbered toward the conference room. As they entered they glanced at the clock. Some slumped in their chairs. Some of them yawned. Boredom was in the air. It was now five minutes beyond the appointed conference time. A few more yawns. Finally the sales manager came in. He carried a handful of papers.

The point: Was it possible that this conference had been called merely for the record? If so, let the record show that a sales conference was held, that it convened late, that 31 salesmen attended, that the sales manager presided, that he spoke in a general way about the current market outlook. He also mentioned the revised vacation schedule. Let the record also show that the sales manager dwelt briefly on the difficulty of developing sales volume "in this slow season." Adjourned.

Let us now get this straight: Unless the sales conference you call is well planned, unless it has a definite objective, unless it has a productive purpose, unless it is well conducted, unless you intend to introduce into it a persuasive spirit, then you should never call that conference.

When salesmen are called to a conference they might reasonably expect that they will be exposed to new ideas from which they might individually profit.

Sales conferences fall into three categories:

1. The dreary, slow-moving, disjointed sessions which generate no sales producing enthusiasm.

2. The social hour session. In this, back-slapping is a major activity. There is much laughter about Joe's luck on the golf course or about the way Charlie panned out in a poker game. There may even be an incidental reference to "a piece of good luck" which yielded a substantial slice of business for Frank. He received little credit among the boys for persuasive selling in landing this business. Just one of those lucky breaks, you understand.

3. The dynamic sales conference gets off on time with enthusiasm. A dynamic sales manager quickly sets up a target and opens fire on it. He maintains continuous fire on this target, which is the primary purpose of the conference. When he gets his point across he terminates discussion. The conference winds up with something definite accomplished, an objective attained. This was all in the mind of the sales manager before he called the conference. He presented a problem. He suggested a solution. He encouraged free discussion. He sold the overall idea. He got everybody enthusiastic about it because he related problem and solution to the pocket books of the salesmen. He adjourned the session ahead of scheduled time at the height of the enthusiasm which he had generated by masterful leadership.

The persuasive sales conference requires dynamic leadership to be successful. Few spots in the sales arena require so much in leadership as the sales conference. A late start can throw cold water on the whole session. A prompt opening with a flash of showmanship arouses attention, stops the yawns. A dynamic opening statement can jar men into thinking and acting. When you rap the gavel you have no time for meditating. Keep it rolling! Make it persuasive!

The planning of, and the conducting of the sales conference is an exercise in the art of persuasion in sales management. By advance thinking and preparation, by definition of purpose and objectives, the sales conference can become a "tool" with which dynamic sales management carves out programs to yield greater sales volume.

Drafting a Persuasive Conference Plan

A sales conference which turns out to be inspiring, persuasive and productive is the product of thoughtful preliminary planning. The foundation for such a conference is the *agenda*. The simplest definition of an agenda is this: "A list of things to be done." If an executive, planning a conference, takes these five steps in preparing his agenda he can make that conference persuasive, and, hopefully, productive:

1. Take time to reduce the purpose of the conference to a brief, easily understood statement. Example: "Today we will introduce to you our newest product, which we believe has high sales potential." Or, "This conference has been called to ask you how we can eliminate certain errors which are picking your pockets and dipping into company profits."

2. Take time to work up a persuasive theme for the session. Example: "New sales goals and how we can reach them" . . . "New and more productive sales techniques and how we can master them and get paid for it" . . . "Adding to your sales volume by developing new accounts and how to do it."

3. Take time to look at the record and to choose someone on the selling team who merits special mention. Individual recognition motivates others to go and do likewise—or better. This is the art of persuasion in action.

4. Take time to make well-chosen assignments for one or two men on the selling team to tell the sales force how they landed a big order or developed a new account.

5. Provide time to listen to ideas from the sales team and to hear suggestions for improvement.

The agenda can play a major role in making your sales conference more productive. The agenda becomes a working plan for the meeting. It provides you with a lever for controling time-wasters. It charts a route to follow to arrive at a given point in your deliberations.

A sales conference aimed at productive results requires:

1. *An agenda* and adherence to it.

2. *Clear-cut definition of purpose* which answers this question: "Why was this conference called?"

3. *Begin on time* with a spirited opening. Avoid monotony. Pack the agenda with persuasive topics which have personal interest for those who attend.

4. *Adjourn on time* and on a high note of enthusiasm.

Be Specific: Clearly Define Your Target

To eliminate foggy thinking which can doom a sales conference to failure do the persuasive thing: *Be specific.*

If you are specific about what you want to accomplish your sales team will be impressed. It's a matter of leadership. Many sales conferences are highly productive because they are well organized and the main idea of the session is clear and persuasive. Sales conferences become highly productive when executive leadership gets right down to the roots of an issue. When sales managers expose these roots and all of their possibilities for their sales teams they get action.

When a sales team "buys" an idea sales volume climbs. As a sales manager your objective is to get your sales team to open fire on the target you have set up for them to shoot at. You are after group action. You want and need the strength of each salesman on your force. Your target must, therefore have a personal, persuasive appeal for each of those salesmen. As Robert Blanchford once wrote: "In all great military and commerical enterprises individualism has to be subordinated to collective action."

An exhibit may assist you in being specific. Your product, a graph, a photograph, or a blackboard gives you something tangible to "talk to." These aids fix audience attention on the point you are attempting to make. They assist you in clarifying and thereby becoming more persuasive.

In virtually every situation which motivates a sales group there is an underlying problem. This simple three-point formula may assist you in giving specific purpose to your conference:

1. The Problem—Define it clearly. One effective sales manager in the electronics field said: "If there is no apparent problem I create one. A problem is the food on which salesmen thrive. If I earnestly desire a 10% jump in sales volume I have a problem. It's that simple. Why beat around the bush about it? Why not get down to business and solve that problem? I get my whole sales team involved in that problem at once. I do this by selling them on the idea that this whole package is directly related to their own self-interest."

2. What Makes it a Problem?—If sales are down, there must be a reason. If sales have leveled off there must be a reason why they didn't climb. Find the reason and you are on your way to constructive action. Get your sales team in on the act of solving your sales problems.

3. Solutions—Waste no time at this point. As a starter for group thinking suggest a solution. Get reaction. Use a blackboard. Write down proposed solutions so the sales team can see the whole picture. With many solutions and the problem there before them you get reaction. They're thinking. You have them involved. Keep the discussion on the track and steer it straight for your target.

Make your sales conference a laboratory in which you can test your salesmanship, your persuasive power. The sales manager of a large department store said: "I never knowingly permit one retail sales person to leave one of my conferences in doubt. I strive to be clear—to have everybody understand what we expect, why we expect it, and how this policy affects their income and their self-interest in its broadest terms. As I see it, as sales manager, it is my job to sell them on ideas through which they and this store can benefit. If I do this job well then it becomes their job and their desire to sell more merchandise."

A Dominating Theme Generates Thinking

Let us assume that you, an ambitious, imaginative, and creative sales manager, have called a sales conference to explain to your sales team how you believe they can make more money for themselves. This should "hook" them. You have a theme. You have something which usually appeals to most men, and also to women. That "thing" is *money*. And, money appeals to them because it's in their self-interest that they have more of it. At least that is the prevailing idea. Now, when you tie this interest to persuasive power you have a winning theme for your sales conference.

This, then, becomes your theme: "How to increase my sales volume and cash in on it."

To do anything with that theme, to make it a reality and not a flimsy dream, you and members of your selling team will have to do some thinking. A dominating theme usually is an assist to thinking. But we don't want to make the mistake of having everybody think as you do. Or, do we? Walter Lippman said: "When all think alike no one thinks very much." Doesn't that seem to be reasonable? It's so easy to agree or to disagree. But to get down to thoughtful digging, that's different. When you are required to concentrate on a specific theme for your next conference *think.*

Henry Ford, an industrialist who must have known a great deal about the subject said: "Thinking is the hardest work there is, which is the probable reason why so few engage in it."

Previously we set up the importance of the agenda as a tool for conducting effective sales conferences. Now let us precede the agenda with a theme. Let us have something on which to base an agenda. A theme, as you know, is simply a topic to be discussed. And, when we have a specific topic we can concentrate. We are persuaded to do some solid thinking. In that way we work around to what our problem really amounts to, and we discover why we have that problem. So, we develop a desire to cope with the problem. You see, we are now getting nearer to our objective. We are getting to the core of our theme. But, it was the theme which got our thinking on the right track. Our theme hasn't changed. This is still it: "How to increase my sales volume and cash in on it."

Several sales managers have suggested such themes as these for their sales conferences:

—How to double current sales of our newest product.
—How to find time for personal development and make sales gains as a result.
—How to uncover new accounts and how to sell them.
—How imagination can open new areas for sales gains.
—How new products for the year can make salesmen richer.

The source of sales conference themes are seemingly endless. Their chief value is in their persuasive content. Themes which are chosen by a sales manager for his conferences may reflect his own creative thinking and reveal his strength of persuasive leadership. Arthur W. Newcomb once observed: "The character and qualifications of a leader are reflected in the men he selects, *develops,* and gathers around him." The effective theme is the one which develops salesmen and motivates them to "reach for the sky" in selling.

Your sales conferences can be made more persuasive by injecting into the theme of each conference that magic element known as persuasion. When this element is coupled with self-interest a sales person begins to *think* in terms of building profitable sales volume. Then it becomes a winner!

To Capture Attention Create Eager Wants

When your sales people file into your conference room you are on a spot. You are in a position similar to that of the teacher who is observing his students entering the classroom. He is looking for some indication of an eager want for learning. The challenge to him is the same as it is to you: How do you get them to listen?

If you talk to your sales people about making more money they'll snap to attention. There's no secret about why. They just want more money and they'll listen to you if you'll tell them how to get it.

When you get down to it sales management is a teaching job. It is also a test in leadership. If you dodge this test you lose persuasive power in your sales team. So, when your sales team responds to your conference call your primary objective is to get their attention. To do this you capitalize on their wants for more money. The more wants they have the more fertile your field for developing selling power.

To create eager wants in your sales team and to get positive action to satisfy those wants try this at your next sales meeting:

Sell them on selling. Build up salesmanship as a prestigious calling which has unlimited financial possibilities. Prove your point by giving them evidence of what other top volume producers are accomplishing with your lines. Show them how they can get into top bracket incomes. Use the power in the art of persuasion to create within your sales people eagerness to become highly paid producers in the field.

Sell them on the products of your firm. Sell them on the possibilities for personal fortune for these who sell those products in volume. Make your appeal factual. Make it alluring. Be so serious and persuasive about this that your sales people will want to get out and overpower any competition. Make your appeal on a personal basis. This is persuasion.

Sell the supporting power of any advertising campaign which has been launched to stimulate demand for your products. Show what promotion is being done. Relate this promotion to their own self-interest. Show how this promotion can mean extra dollars in the pockets of each member of your selling team. Create desire within them to get their full share of this generated market demand.

The point is this: If your sales people can be made to want more money and want it badly enough they'll go after it in the market place, and they'll get it.

The result: You will be crowned as a dynamic sales manager, all because you employed the power of persuasion in sales managment to get productive action.

When you rap the starting gavel at your next sales conference be aware of this fact: *You are now on display! Do something about it!*

You have preached the doctrine of positive action to your sales people. Now try it on yourself. You have sounded off to your sales people that the first three minutes in the presence of a prospect are crucial in making a sale. You have told them to go after the prospect's attention and to hold on to it when they get attention. Now try that doctrine yourself. Try it out on your sales team. It's sound doctrine. It pays off.

Apathy is a serious threat in any sales conference. Apathy produces yawns. Arnold Toynbee, the British educator, hit the nail on the head when he said: "Apathy can only be overcome by enthusiasm, and enthusiasm can only be aroused by two things; first an ideal which takes the imagination by storm, and second, a definite intelligible plan for carrying that ideal into practice."

To capture attention of your sales team present a specific idea. Dress up that idea so that it will be enticing. When you see the eyes of your sales people light up, you are on the right track. When you see them eagerly making notes during your presentation you have hit a responsive chord. You probably have created within them an eager want for something. Stay with it now! By constant persuasion you can capitalize on their wants and thereby develop sales volume. The sure way to hold their attention is to feed their eagerness so that their wants will grow.

Let Them Tell You How to Solve the Problem

The advertising director of a metropolitan daily newspaper had a problem. One of the most desirable retail accounts in his area was cold on newspaper advertising. This merchant was putting his fat promotion budget into TV, radio, billboards and direct mail. The newspaper sales manager had no difficulty defining his objective: To get that merchant's advertising into his newspaper.

This executive presented the problem to his sales team. "Just how have we been missing the boat?" he asked his sales people. "How can we persuade this man to use newspaper advertising?" He had passed the ball to his sales staff and the response was immediate and favorable. The salesmen had some positive ideas on how to reach that merchant. This sales manager had in that single gesture accomplished three things:

1. He had involved his entire staff in a major problem. He had presented this problem in a persuasive manner. He had appealed to the pride and self-interest of his staff.
2. He had secured from his staff more than 50 solid suggestions on how one unsold merchant probably could be persuaded to revise his advertising advertising policy and test the pulling power of the newspaper.
3. He proved that a sales conference can be made both persuasive and profitable.

The massive sales pressure built up by this advertising director within his sales staff eventually resulted in the merchant's advertising appearing in the columns of that newspaper.

The secret of this sales executive's accomplishment: He recognized the combined ability in his staff. This appealed to the ego of his men. He capitalized on pride. He asked them how to get a job done and they told him, which was much more effective than if he had attempted to convince them.

What this sales manager was doing was simply using the persuasive power in humility. He shifted the spotlight from himself to his staff. Doing this he implied that they were very important people. In effect he was saying to them: "I believe you know all about problems such as this, now you tell me what is the best way to solve it." This involved each one of those salespeople in a major project and it paid off because his approach had all of the elements of effective persuasion.

Prearranged Talks by the Staff Have Persuasive Possibilities

To spice up your sales conferences and to make them more persuasive get off the platform and let the salesmen have a fling at taking over. You can do this by thoughtful advance planning. Select salesmen to make talks. Challenge them to say something that will benefit their colleagues. What they say may even be enlightening to you as sales manager. Within reason give them a free hand in expression. In assigning these talks keep these four points in mind:

1. Three talks for one session are sufficient. Too many and too long is too much. Five minutes each is sufficient for greatest impact.
2. Choose speakers who are representative of the sales team in experience. For example: A veteran salesman, another with about one year's experience, and a third by a newcomer to the staff. Subjects might be: For the veteran: "How I have profited in today's market by what I learned years ago in selling." For the one-year salesman: "My toughest sale and how I handled it." For the newcomer: "How I propose to increase my sales volume next month."
3. When these three salesmen have spoken you take over again and you summarize what has been said. Then open the session for questions directed at the three speakers. Let them answer the questions. In this way you involve the whole selling team.
4. Relate the three talks to the overall theme of your conference whenever possible.

The sales team of one sales executive in the communication field made his conferences so interesting and valuable that his staff looked forward to each session. He kept the team guessing about what he would spring on them. He used speakers from the team about once a month. He held weekly conferences. "I believe sales conferences must carry a punch or it's wasted time," he said. "If I can keep my sales people guessing about what is coming next I have made yardage. This virtually assures that I will get response. It enlivens the conference. When the staff is fully keyed up I find that I can get across my point more effectively."

Successful sales conferences are successful because some sales executive planned them that way. Such sales executives constantly fight against mediocrity in their staffs. They seem to have a permanent objective: "To do better than the best that has already been done."

Charles H. Brower, business executive, left this warning note for those who aspire to greatness in selling:

"Here in America we have reached the high tide of mediocrity, the era of the great goof-off, the age of the half-done job." He pointed an accusing finger at executives whose minds are on the golf course instead of on the market and on selling. He chided students who take cinch courses because the hard ones make them think. He could have included those who call themselves salesmen but, for want of persuasive executive direction and motivation, do not sell with full persuasive vigor.

Persuasive Value of the Question Box

A textile operator placed question boxes in various departments of his plant. One was in a spot handy for salesmen. One was near each drinking fountain. "Why?" asked one of his assistants. "Ideas," replied the operator of those mills. "We need fresh ideas. Questions stimulate thinking and thinking produces ideas."

In sales management the question box can have persuasive value. Among salesmen it often stimulates imaginative thinking. To make the question box productive it may require a degree of salesmanship. It is another idea that must be sold to the sales team to get response. But, if you publicly commend one of your salesmen for submitting a constructive idea you'll notice other salesmen begin thinking and submitting questions and suggestions.

The question box (or suggestion box) has two purposes in sales management:

To get ideas which can be converted into sales via the sales conference route.

To get an appraisal of the quality of thinking in the sales staff. Questions and suggestions from the sales staff often reflect that you have an untapped reservoir of creative and constructive thinking which can be turned into sales volume via the sales conference route. Albert Einstein, the scientist, rated imagination high in value. "Imagination is more important than knowledge," he said. Creative and imaginative ideas often appear in suggestion boxes.

Through exploitation the question or suggestion box can become a conversation piece for your sales staff. This generates thinking. Imagination is stimulated. Ideas result. This provides fuel for productive sales conferences. When sales management takes note of a question box idea the word spreads and this activates others to contribute to "the box." Suddenly the question box becomes popular. It becomes a persuasive instrument—a device for developing sales volume. This results from imaginative exploitation of "the box."

This is the art of persuasion in sales management. But neither the question box, nor any other device for sales team involvement, will survive and become productive without *persuasive nourishment.*

How to Stir Up Mass Enthusiasm

Mass enthusiasm should be the objective of every purposeful sales conference. For instance:

(a) We have a new product.
(b) We can see a growing market in our territory for that product.
(c) This product, being new, will require hard selling.

Our problem: To present this product and its possibilities in a way that will excite our sales teams.

Solution of the problem: (a) To show the product and demonstrate how it is made, or how it works, or how it is used; (b) to demonstrate how this product will be beneficial to buyers—how it affects buyers personally; (c) to present a persuasive and uncomplicated selling plan to the selling team. To show how salesmen can dramatize the product. To show how they can put excitement into their demonstrations and sales presentations. To show how they can get prospects excited about the product and its possibilities for benefiting them.

Caution: Before attempting to stir up mass enthusiasm in your selling team be sure that you are fired up about your sales idea and about your product to the point where you want to get into the harness yourself and get out in the field and sell it. Then you are conditioned to stir up mass enthusiasm in others. You can't be lukewarm on this deal. You have to be hot. "Nothing great was ever achieved without enthusiasm," wrote Ralph Waldo Emerson. This may bring to mind the sales executive who droned out announcements in sales conferences and was disappointed when his proposals fell flat with his sales team. On this point, Earl Nightingale, a business executive, had this thought: "Get a person happily excited about something and you've got an enthusiastic person on your hands. Get happily excited about something yourself and you'll be enthusiastic."

Success of your sales conference depends upon how much enthusiasm you generate about your problem. As one discerning sales executive put it: "If I have a concrete purpose in calling a conference then I have the basic substance for enthusiasm. If I have thought over this thing well and if I have devised a program for that conference which will focus attention on my product, and if I have made this exciting, and if I make this presentation appealing to each member of my sales team, then I can reasonably expect some measure of success out of that conference."

The secret of creating mass enthusiasm is excitement within yourself. Enthusiasm is the most contagious thing in the world. Sales records are built upon enthusiasm. It is the essence of the art of persuasion in sales management.

The Time-Saving Art in Conducting Sales Conferences

A sales manager in the insurance and investment field became widely known as a dynamic leader. To sit in on one of this executive's sales conferences was a lesson in time-saving. He accomplished more in 30 minutes than most executives accomplish in an hour or more. He had a formula for getting things done by the most direct route. This was his sales conference formula:

1. Announce why the conference was called. Make it brief, clear, specific, persuasive.
2. Present the problem. State how and why it affects each member of the sales staff.
3. Invite staff members to offer suggested solutions of the problem.
4. Invite brief remarks from the staff on (a) the problem, and (b) on solutions that have been suggested. Permit no diversionary discussion.
5. Summarize. Announce decision or state that the staff will be advised later of the executive decision. Adjourn.

Sales conferences become productive in ideas and persuasive in action power when the presiding executive: (a) shows respect for the value of time; (b) holds a tight rein on discussion; (c) keeps discussion moving steadily toward the primary objective of the conference.

The sales director of an advertising agency had his own time-saving method: "I open my conferences with a *provocative problem*. I find it quite simple to dig out a provocative problem from the subject matter scheduled for the discussion. With the provocative problem out in the open, wheels begin turning in various heads in the group at the conference table. When I call for ideas about solving the problem I get response. Only after the staff has spoken do I inject my wisdom into the discussion. By this time we have worked out some sort of constructive plan and I wrap up the session. To me conference planning is one of the most important functions of an executive. Unless conferences are well-planned and well-handled they are time-wasters. As executives, I believe we must keep in mind that a one hour conference with ten salesmen present represents ten hours of selling time—more than a normal day's work for one salesman. That's a big investment. We should make it pay off."

In sales management the allied arts of time-saving and persuasion yield high dividends in production. When mastered the art of time-saving and the art of persuasion are marks of distinction, even of greatness, in dynamic sales executives.

Idea + People + Persuasive Influence = More Sales

Look at your sales conference as a link in a communication chain which successful sales managers cling to in attaining their goals of greater and more profitable sales volume. Consider this sales communication chain in this light:

1. *The Beginning*—An idea.
2. *Who's Concerned?*—People.
3. *How Can I Reach Them?*—Through the art of persuasion.
4. *What Happens?*—Increased sales volume.

These are four relatively simple steps and yet they define the importance of the communication chain in sales management.

In sales management an idea may relate to a product or to a certain technique in selling. The idea may be an intangible thing. It may, however, relate to something tangible. In either event an idea is something we must deal with in sales management.

We are dealing with people. We begin with our sales staffs. Each member of our sales staff will have prospects with whom he must deal. In turn they will develop into established customers with whom the salesman must deal. To do this successfully salesmen must know about people, how to get along with them, and how to persuade them to buy.

You, as sales manager, also must deal with people. Your salesmen require persuasive prodding to get them excited about selling in greater volume. You, too, must know about people, how to handle them and how each member of your sales team will probably react in a given situation. That is what is expected of you as a sales manager. You even expect this of yourself.

Persuasive influence is a power which causes people to act. Sales managers and salesmen use this art in influencing others. People buy because salesmen persuade them to buy. Salesmen react favorably to sales management persuasion because they have become convinced that they will benefit by falling into line and producing more.

When sales managers and their sales teams pick up every link in the sales communication chain and get those links hooked together and when there is no weak link in the chain between the inception of the idea and the closing of the sale then sales management and selling teams, working together, have made constructive headway.

The sales conference can also be made more persuasive by holding on to a similar line of communication. By calling a conference with a definite purpose in mind, by presenting a provocative idea, by knowing how to get people (your sales staff) excited about your idea, you are in position to apply persuasive influence upon your sales staff. As a result, if your chain of communication is strong in every link you will get more sales out of your sales conferences.

This is the art of persuasion in selling, in sales management and also in presiding over sales conferences. It is the most important link in that chain of communication extending from the inception of a sales idea to the closing of the sale. It is the art of communication in sales management.

chapter 14

How to Fire Up
Your Sales Staff
with Selling Power

When we set out to find ways and means of firing up our sales teams we intimate that the art of persuasion in sales management is a dynamic power. The fact is that the art of persuasion gets down to the root of a problem. It stimulates action.

The art of persuasion reaches a high potential when those in sales management and those who sell are fired up with a zealous desire to roll up sales volume in the face of the most obstinate opposition. This power, thus generated, relates specifically to people. It involves all who are involved in producing sales. In substance it is that quality which we refer to as "selling power." That power is wrapped up in the sales techniques of master salesmen and dynamic sales managers.

To fire up sales teams to their highest productive heat the following five points are suggested.

Health

Ailing sales managers usually fall short in leadership in today's competitive market. They lack the spark which fires up sales people to establish and maintain high sales records. By the same token, ailing salesmen invariably fall short of their sales goals. The ailing person lacks spirit. His aching belly, his throbbing head, or his creaking joints apply brakes to his sales efforts.

Good health is the blessing of life. It also pays high dividends. To keep their bodies and their minds in fighting condition wise sales managers and their salesmen remain on speaking terms with their doctors. They go in for checkups regularly. They do what the medic tells them to do. They capitalize on staying well, rather than getting well, whenever that is possible. If a sales manager or a salesman is constitutionally unfit to stand up under the stress of today's pressures he should be rational about it and make appropriate adjustments. But, if the human machine is in working order and a sales manager and a salesman keep it that way, they can profit and perhaps avoid a major overhaul of that machine. By doing this they become more persuasive personalities. This raises the question: How long has it been since you had a thorough physical checkup? This is often the first step necessary to getting fired up with greater persuasive power in dynamic sales management.

Zeal

You have seen zealous sales managers who have been supercharged with enthusiasm. These executives inspired their selling teams with zealousness, unless they were an exception to the rule. Zeal seems to be a spiritual quality which can be developed by dedicated interest. Evangelists have this sort of zeal. Dynamic sales managers have it. By zealousness these sales managers sway their sales people to "reach for the skies" in sales production. Zealousness is closely related to the art of persuasion. George Romney, master automobile salesman, executive and politician, once said: "Man cannot separate his spiritual life from his social, political and economic life and remain free."

Purpose

Too often we head out into the open with no destination in mind. After a few miles interest lags. Then we encounter unforeseen difficulties. A road block stops our progress. We take off on a questionable detour. We get on a steep, narrow mountain road. We see the summit ahead. Our interest becomes keen. But, then a spark plug in our car fails. Now we really perk up. Purpose has been injected into our purposeless trip. And, so it is quite often in business. With an established goal, with purpose, a sales campaign often develops power on its own fuel. Without purpose a whole sales campaign has been known to collapse. Define your purpose.

Define that purpose clearly and persuasively to your sales people. Show them the goal that you have established. Get them fired up as you are. Point out to them how they can profit by zealously and persuasively selling whatever it is that you have to sell. This is the art of persuasion which dynamic sales managers have found to be so successful.

Action

A fisherman rarely gets fired up by watching a sluggish stream. A sluggish stream is a lazy man's delight. To sales people a sluggish presentation by their sales manager ignites no fires within them. Sales people rise to the persuasive power of zeal and purpose. Dynamic sales managers put zeal and purpose into their presentations to get results in terms of greater sales volume. Action is persuasive in itself. The forward movement stirs up interest. Action is the end product of the art of persuasion in sales management.

Speak Up

To transmit the fire within you to your sales people, speak up! A sales executive's voice can be a remarkably effective tool with great persuasive power. Mumblers rarely get you excited, do they? But thunder does! The man whose voice is heard loud and clear by the man seated in the last row in the conference room has one up on the man who speaks in modulated tones. You can train your voice so you will be heard. You can cultivate speaking habits which will add to your persuasive power. The principle: With hearing goes listening, and with listening comes opportunity for effective persuasion. At your next sales conference speak out with fervor and note what happens in your sales people. Speaking to be heard and listened to is also closely related to the art of persuasion in sales management and also in salesmanship.

A sales manager in the tire industry established a reputation for firing up his sales people with selling power. He explained his technique in this way:

"There isn't anything artificial in the way I stir up my selling team. I'm sincere when I push them for action. I'm serious and sincere when I point out their weaknesses to them. I'm selfishly sincere when I detail to them how they can do a better job. There are times, however, when I feel that I am short on sincerity. That time is when my purpose is not clearly defined. When that happens I have a positive remedy. I jump right into the middle of the problem myself. I pick up a sales kit and get out in the field, working with my people. There I observe, listen and ask questions. I find

out about consumer likes and dislikes. I find out about dealer reactions to
our product. This firsthand knowledge is persuasive stuff. It gives me the
drive to go after my sales people with a purpose, to fire them up with
selling power."

The Sales Power of Health Plus Persuasion

At the close of a presentation meeting in which awards were given to
a group of salesmen for notable achievement the star sales producer of the
group was rushed by newspaper men who asked him:

"To what do you give credit for your success in landing the top
award on this occasion?"

The salesman replied:

"First to my good health. And, next to my sales manager who
inspired me to go after business in a big way."

Note the persuasive factors in this salesman's reply: (a) good health
and (b) the spirit of achievement. The health factor he placed at the top
of the list.

We have become a health conscious nation. But, then, health has
persuasive power. Some sales managers and salesmen have joined what is
called "health food groups." With them diet has become a persuasive
factor. It is not our purpose here to discuss the merits of such diets but to
make this point: When a sales executive becomes unduly conscious of his
physical well-being he is apt to sacrifice persuasive qualities which he
requires to inspire and motivate his selling team. As you will see, there is a
close relationship between health and persuasive power. Your executive
success depends upon mastering the art of persuasion in sales management. Good health will hasten your success in mastering that art.

The importance of health to the sales executive was recognized by
Samuel Johnson when he wrote: "Health is, indeed, so necessary to all
duties as well as pleasures of life that the crime of squandering it is equal
to the folly."

At times we are told that we are working too hard. We are told by
anxious friends and members of our families to "slow down." We
rightfully wonder whether "slowing down" will accomplish its desired
purpose. Otto Graham, former gridiron pro and football coach, had
firsthand knowledge about physical fitness and its persuasive power over
others. He had this advice for the "take it easy" advocates:

"Part of our trouble," said Graham, "can be traced to the popular
philosophy of: 'Let's take it easy.' "

The sales manager has a dual responsibility in health preservation.

First he has the responsibility of developing sales in volume. To accomplish this he needs the stimulating power which accompanies good health. He also has the responsibility of developing selling power in his sales people. To achieve this end he has the responsibility of persuading them to keep fit physically and mentally.

Sales are better developed by men with healthy bodies and keen minds. Sales people who are free of the depressing effects of chronic ailments are more persuasive. Freedom from pain and from worry enables them to "reach for the skies" in selling. The sales manager's dual objective is this: (a) To keep fit himself; (b) to persuade his sales team to keep fit. Preventive medicine is a good investment in sales management.

The private secretary of one highly rated sales executive passed on this office "secret" to another executive:

"My boss takes a nap every afternoon, just after lunch. He relaxes for about 30 minutes. That's why I won't disturb him right now. You ought to try it. You know, my boss rarely has a sick day."

While the daily nap is generally accepted as a sensible idea it has been known to develop extremists. One of such extremists suggested that a short nap more than compensated for a full night's sleep. Of course sleep is something the insomniac might desire more than sales volume. A physician explained the predicament of some insomniacs: "They don't relax," he said. "They get to worrying about not sleeping and this worry keeps them awake. Until they can so discipline themselves that they learn the trick of relaxing they'll have wakeful nights." To this we might add that they probably will continue to have problems, if they are sales executives, and this may add to their sleeplessness. Problems are part of the life of sales managers and, yet, even sales managers can make allowances to enjoy restful sleep.

Here are five suggested methods by which sales managers might get brief snatches of sleep to refresh the taxed human system:

1. A midday nap at a regular time, shut off from interruption.
2. Recline in a comfortable chair with feet elevated to hip level.
3. A warm bath or a brief rest in a steam room.
4. Eat moderately. Avoid eating when under severe pressure or tension.
5. Take a break from your desk. Walk around a block. Refresh yourself with a cold drink (non-alcoholic).

Health Principle: Take time out to relax.

The sales manager of a marine equipment enterprise became known as "the clean-up executive." He meticulously cleared his desk of pressing problems before he quit for the day. To do this he held to a three-point rule:

1. "I make no night decisions. I find that morning decisions are best. My mind is clearer then. I am refreshed then, or, at least I should be.
2. "I take up undesirable tasks first. I get them out of the way. I have found that dodging unpleasant duties takes more energy than doing them. Just looking at those tasks with dread is fatiguing.
3. "I tackle tough problems first. I get a feeling of strength by solving them. This refuels me for going after the other problems. I suggest you try it."

Golden Briggs, a business executive who no doubt has seen other executives and sales people punish their minds and bodies offered this horse-sense health suggestion:

"Invest at least 15 minutes of each day to physical toning up of your body."

When you combine the glow of health with the art of persuasion you have a magic formula for dynamic sales management.

How Sales Records Fall Victims of Hypochondria

Hypochondriac salesmen are rated high as sales killers. There is little mystery about how their "crimes" are committed. This is how they work:

1. They begin by shattering the nerves of sales managers who are striving to make them persuasive sales people.
2. They cough and sniffle in the presence of the sales manager and also in the presence of prospective buyers.
3. They often interrupt a sales presentation to gulp a pill.
4. They expound to prospective buyers about their many ills. They seldom get really sick. They just annoy.
5. They dwell on their physical woes, thus driving prospective buyers and associates away from them.

The sales director of an expanding building construction enterprise eliminated hypochondriacs from his selling team. This is how he identified them early enough to prevent them from "contaminating" his sales staff:

They were among the salesmen who habitually dragged into the conference room a few minutes late each morning.

They were the ones who became obnoxious by discussing their "suffering." This sales manager reasoned that if they would do this in the office they would do it in the field and that in doing that they would become potential sales killers.

They were those who, when asked why they did not consult a physician, came back at their sales manager with an imposing list of specialists whom they had already consulted. They bemoaned the fact that all of those specialists had given them a physical O.K., but they were still "sick."

They were those who knew all about diseases, treatments, medical terms and about quacks as well as about ethical medical practitioners, and who had intense interest in all the faddist treatments for all ailments.

The dictionary defines hypochondria as "unnecessary anxiety about one's health; imaginary illness; low spirits without any real reason." Those definitions lack persuasive power. But, we find in the hypochondriac the power to repell. Hypochondria can attack sales managers as well as salesmen. When it does it compounds the killing effect on sales records.

You may have met a sales manager who had a drug assortment in his office. His private drug store probably included a "miracle remedy" for virtually every ailment in the book, including gas on the stomach, a headache, and a pain in the neck.

Hypochondria is a threat to sales volume gains. We can turn back to the "mirror trick" in our search for probable causes of some sales slumps. Many sales managers practice psychiatry without a license. They do it in this way: They may call a chronically sniffling salesman into the executive office. There they lay the law down to him—"shape up or ship out." Such sales managers have become fed up with self-pity. They have heard enough of excuses for sales losses and too little about sales gains. When they have exploded they have startled hypochrondriacal sales people. Never before have they been talked to as that sales manager talked to them. This experience had been different from going from physician to physician searching for a sound reason for selling less and less. Such hard-nosed sales managers usually prescribe a new treatment for the hypochondriac: Sell or move over and make room for those who are not overanxious about health and who are definitely anxious about building sales volume. With some of the hypochondriacs this treatment has been effective. With some it has shaken them up so they have "miraculously" recovered from their ills. And they have gone out in the field where they had fallen down before and they have come back with satisfactory sales records.

In some instances hypochrondria is a form of fear, according to some authorities on emotional disorders. Hypochondriacs live in fear of disease. They use symptoms of disease as excuses for bad performance as sales people. Then they become fearful of losing their jobs, and of losing status in business, in society, and even in their homes. Hypochondria is not only a sales killer, it is an all around wrecker of potentially capable people.

One medical authority estimates that more than 50% of patients going to family physicians are victims of emotional rather than physical disorder. Included in that 50% are some hypochondriacs. Among the hypochondriacs are some sales people, also some sales managers, who are holding down sales production.

Check the following reasons for poor sales records. Note those which may have a familiar ring:

"What ails you?"—"Nothing serious. Just nerves."

"This was a bad selling day for me. The whole world seemed to be against me. I haven't felt well for days. You can't do much about that, can you?"

"Headaches? Man, do I get headaches! The doctor has given me everything in the book, but I still get them. Terrible! Believe me it's tough to try to sell with a throbbing head. Maybe I need more rest?"

"Indigestion? It sure gets me. Must be something I eat. I've tried switching my diet. When that doesn't help, I try some of those remedies I hear about on TV. Maybe I'm working too hard?"

One medical authority declares that it is rare to find an individual who is perfectly healthy. This may be encouraging to some hypochondriacs. To others it may be disappointing. It does knock out one idea: That hypochondriacs are in a privileged class.

The same medical authority pointed out that the majority of people have some irritations, some minor pains and some aches, but they do not make a fuss about them. Instead, they concentrate on getting a job done. It's when sniffles and muscle spasms and creaking joints are magnified into boring proportions that they become sales killers.

The sales manager of a drug firm had an exceptionally low record of absenteeism in his sales staff due to illness. Someone lightly suggested that this probably was due to the lines they carried which included a drug for most ailments. However, the sales manager denied that this had a bearing on the record of his sales staff. He gave this as the reason for the favorable record:

"I pile on each salesman a few more assignments every day than I think he can handle. This amounts to persuasive pressure. In a sense it shows that I have confidence in the person so challenged. The interesting thing is that they get the job done, and our sales volume goes up. I believe the effectiveness of this method is that it gives the sales person little time to think about his personal woes, his minor aches, or his pains. They become more interested in their work by being challenged in a way that indicates that their sales manager believes in them."

Apparently the art of persuasion in sales management has been effectively used as a remedy for hypochondria and resulted in building sales volume.

Relationship of Bicarbonate of Soda to Sales Curves

One of the prevalent afflictions of those who work in the pressure chambers of business is indigestion. This ailment takes in a broad field, all the way from the distress of acid indigestion to the torture of a full-blown ulcer. It accounts for high consumption of bicarbonate of soda and the more sophisticated remedies for ailing stomachs.

Tonight your TV screen will probably bring you up to date on what progress has been made in developing remedies for digestive disorders. Among the prospective customers for these disorders are sales managers, sales people, advertising agency executives, and other high strung creative persons. These people work in the pressure chamber of business. Most of these people are candidates for membership in the "Ulcer Society."

Symptoms of this prevalent occupational disease which creates a demand for bicarbonate of soda and affects sales curves: (a) persistent heartburn; (b) burning sensation in the pit of the stomach; (c) distress after eating; (d) bellyache that awakens you from sleep, etc.

Common sense convinces us that ulcers, or just an upset stomach, make no contribution to increasing sales volume. This, then, makes it clear why bicarbonate of soda has a relationship to sales curves.

Now that we have enumerated some of the distressing symptoms of this sales killing ailment we might profitably search for the causes of such attacks. Our search might lead us to the most common cause—*nervous tension*. Now we need to understand what may cause nervous tension. Here, then, are three well-known offenders:

1. *Indecision*—Among sales managers we find men of snap judgment, men who make thoughtful decisions and men who grapple under tension with their problems because of indecision. The longer you dodge the issue the tighter your nerves become. Tight nerves throw your digestive machine out of kilter.

2. *Fear*—This is a handicap which you and I prefer to admit affects only other people. However, you and I are in the pressure chamber of business and we do fear, now and then, that we may not make the grade. We fear that things may go haywire. We fear that the economy may slip. We fear that our sales volume may slide. The record shows that most of our fears never materialize, but we still remain fearful. We go right ahead creating new fears. We find a new way to throw a monkey wrench into our digestive apparatus. This causes us agony and this contributes to a decline in sales, which creates more tension.

3. *Worry*—This contributor to nervous tension is a master saboteur. It causes your stomach to churn. Liberal doses of bicarbonate of soda are taken to quiet the stomach. Perhaps it did not occur to you at the time but worry may actually have been responsible for your executive sales plans being non-productive. Worry robs sales managers of leadership power. Worry robs sales people of persuasive power. Worry is a threat to health and a threat to success in sales management. Conquer it! It has been done!

The foregoing are the skeletons of three major offenders, all creators of sales killing nervous tension. To subdue these offenders you probably gulped bicarbonate of soda last night and again this morning. You probably neglected to do something which would be more appeasing to your rebellious digestive system. There are three steps which have been tested and which have been effective with men who work under pressure:

1. Work Off Your Tensions—Tone up the body. Combat this distressing and destructive tightness with physical and mental vigor, thus increasing your capacity to lead your sales team and to inspire your sales people to sell through greater persuasive power.
2. Unmask Your Problems—Get your troubles out in the open. Turn the light on them. Stare at them. Get angry about them. Why permit them to cut down your sales volume? Are they really insurmountable, or are you big enough to beat them?
3. Act! Do Something About It!—Don't stand there wringing your hands. It's the worrisome, fearful approach to problems which tightens up your nerves. When you unmask your problems, when you tear into them, when you do something to solve them, it's amazing how tension diminishes.

This is not intended to be a medical treatise on indigestion and what it does to sales volume. On the contrary it is intended as a reminder to sales managers that indigestion and bicarbonate of soda have a direct relationship to sales curves.

To combat indigestion caused by nervous tension many sales managers hold their nerves in check. These sales managers capitalize on their nervous energy by diverting it to creative channels. By controlling this energy these sales managers convert it to productive ideas for increasing sales. In effect these sales managers take control of an unruly, destructive force and make it productive. They also free themselves of the punishment inflicted by rebellious nerves. The secret: "Know thyself."

While bicarbonate of soda may temporarily appease a disorderly digestive system we find no case record to assure us that this product, or any other anti-acid, will miraculously and permanently sweeten the sour stomachs of hard-pressed sales managers and their sales teams. Nor is there convincing evidence that these remedies will correct a decline in sales volume which has resulted from lack of persuasive selling. On the other hand there is evidence that in many cases the art of persuasion in sales management has been so productive that the demand for bicarbonate of soda has sharply declined.

Tips for Generating a Fighting Spirit in Timid Sales People

In timidity sales management is dealing with fear. This can be either a negative or a positive force in selling. Fear motivates many to buy. We have fear of poverty, fear of ill health, fear of bad breath, fear of old age—all factors in selling. But in the timidity of sales people we are dealing with the senseless fear of meeting and talking to people. We are even dealing with the fear of being ourselves. To sell more sales management has a challenge to strengthen the timid who do sincerely want to become successful sales people. These timid souls must first rid themselves of timidity, and this can be done. Consider the following five steps for generating a fighting spirit in timid sales people.

Persuade Them to Express Their Own Needs

The first principle in curbing timidity is to expose a compelling need. If this need, expressed by a timid sales person on your staff, is realistic, then that sales person has presented to you a tangible "something" which has potential persuasive power.

Persuade Them to Eagerly Want Something Which Will Supply Their Needs

The most wanted thing among sales people generally is more money. This want can be supplied through greater sales volume. Few things are as persuasive as wants. When your sales people are persuaded to expose their needs they also reveal their wants. By exposing their needs and declaring their wants they have taken the first step toward breaking the chains of timidity. An eager want can be a powerful driving force. When a salesman gets fully involved in satisfying an eager want he is inclined to forget timidity. Thus, through the persuasive power of an eager want a once timid sales person begins to fight for business. He substitutes courage for fear.

Persuade Them to Establish Goals

To persuade timid sales people to satisfy their needs and their wants challenge them to set up, with your assistance, a realistic goal, and inspire them to go after it. Their target is more money to supply their needs and their wants. Your target is simply to crush the timidity which is holding them back.

Let's take it step by step. Encourage a timid soul to gain a little yardage today. He tastes victory even in a small sale. Tomorrow, with your persuasion, he gains more yardage. Success becomes a persuasive factor in his life. A fighting spirit takes possession of him. He craves more success. Soon timidity is replaced with positive, persuasive action. He sells and he profits. And, so do you. He is now adding to your sales volume. You, too, have tasted of leadership victory through the art of persuasion in sales management.

Persuade Them to Believe in Themselves and in What They Sell

Show your timid sales people how the products they have to sell can yield benefits for them and to those to whom they sell. Show them how they are performing a beneficial service by selling to prospective buyers. Convince them that this is true. Build up their enthusiasm for what they have to sell. Build up their self-confidence. You have the record to support the claims you make. But to stir up a timid sales person's fighting spirit you need to be at the boiling point yourself. Lukewarm sales managers seldom become dynamic sales executives. The art of persuasion provides an effective antidote for the poison of timidity.

Show Them How to Free Themselves of Timidity

You may tell your timid sales people that timidity is foolish, but that is not sufficiently persuasive to enable them to conquer that handicap. You need something to ignite those timid souls with a selling spirit. You can, for instance, show them case records of how others build sales power by fearless action. You can train them to use the art of persuasion in selling. You can motivate them to satisfy their needs and their wants by developing sales volume. You can point out to them why timidity is denying those things to them.

To crush timidity thrust your own enthusiasm and courage into your training program.

Develop self-confidence in your selling team. Favorably recognize the more timid ones for small victories. This has the persuasive effect of leading to greater victories. To crush timidity in your sales people challenge them, individually. Challenge the timid ones to begin climbing to the top of the production list. Point out to them how this can be done, one step at a time. Generate a fighting spirit in timid sales people.

One warning for sales managers: Never, but never make light of a timid sales person. His burden is great enough without adding to it. It's courage and encouragement he needs.

Timidity is a form of fear. You see the dread in the expression in the face of a timid sales recruit who is on his way to match his wits with his first prospect. One dynamic sales manager related how he dreaded making sales contacts when he first entered selling as a career. "My first prospect was assigned to me by my sales manager," he said. "I walked around the block three times before I got up enough courage to go in and see that fellow. The palms of my hands were wet. The prospect's secretary told me her boss was in. This disappointed me. Really, I had wanted to have a valid excuse to get out of there. I entered my prospect's private office and he must have seen that I was shaking. He was kind, however. He broke the ice for me. He told me about the swell outfit I represented. Finally I got into action. I made a feeble presentation of our newest office products. The man I had dreaded seeing went over those products with great care. He asked a lot of questions. He also gave me a substantial order. That is, I thought it was a great order. He also shook my hand and slapped me on the back. This strengthened me. I'll never forget that guy. A few months later he told me that I had put him in mind of himself when he tackled his first prospect. You see, that guy had climbed to his present position by conquering timidity, and he was now teaching others to conquer it. He was a dynamic sales executive. I still rate him as the most dynamic sales manager I have ever met."

It was Sydney Smith who gave us one principle of conquering timidity. This is that principle, which sales managers might well pass on to their timid sales people:

"To do anything in the world worth doing we must not stand back shivering and thinking of the cold and danger, but jump in and scramble through as best we can."

Three-Way Health Balance and Its Persuasive Selling Power

The possibility of your being able to fire up your sales staff with selling power largely depends on the vigor of your sales people. And, of course, that vigor is the product of good health. As a sales manager, you have a selfish motive in promoting good health in your staff. You are primarily interested in developing sales volume. Increased persuasive power in your selling team often springs from those enjoying vigorous health. The following three-way health balance is, therefore, projected for promoting physical and mental fitness in sales people:

1. Develop health habits which will generate selling power.
2. Banish worry to gain greater selling power.
3. Learn to "let down" in order to pick up selling power.

You will note that in the foregoing "Three-Way Health Balance," *habit* is set out as the number one factor. The idea is to get your sales people "hooked" on sound health habits.

If sales people will "eat to live and not live to eat" they may improve in health. The habit of taking on and devouring a doughnut and coffee breakfast in speed-test time is out, although many salesmen have been "hooked" by this habit.

Preventative health care is sound. This entails regular medical checkups. A sound personal preventative health program usually holds down the number of emergency calls on physicians. Preventing disease in sales people has more sales-building power than curing disease.

The habit of "letting down" in order to pick up selling power makes sense. We are told that nature looks with favor on a reasonable amount of rest in order to avoid fatigue. You might encourage your sales people to develop the habit of an occasional "let down" in order to recapture selling power. One of the top producers in consumer product sales developed this habit. On one occasion he had built up tension while closing an involved sale. As he came out of that place of business he paused, took a few deep breaths, mentally ran over what had transpired, threw back his shoulders and walked vigorously toward his car. As he walked he drew in his stomach muscles, flexed the muscles in his arms, and took time to flex the muscles in his legs before he got into his car. Why all this? This is the way he explained it:

"In those three or four minutes I refueled. I refreshed myself physically and mentally. Muscle-flexing is a mild form of exercise. So is posture. In letting down occasionally I accomplish more for my physical and mental well-being than I would by consuming two or three cups of coffee as some of my colleagues do. Moreover, I have saved time. I suggest something like this as a habit for sales managers as well as for their sales people."

The worry bug is a tenacious creature. It saps selling power out of sales people. Those who have studied the worry bug's habits have decided that habit can also subdue this menace to selling power. Some sales people have highly developed worry habits. They worry over sales losses. They worry over sales victories, fretting that they might have done better. Few things discourage the one who has fallen victim of the worry bug from worrying. Sales management might suggest to these people that worrying is an expensive habit. They might point out that worry is a sales killer. They might ask the worrier what is the worst that could possibly happen to him. Ask him, also, if he is strong enough to handle the worst that could happen to him. This sort of challenge may get through to him. But those who are addicted to worrying over trifles must learn to swat the worry bug with their own power, which also goes for worrying sales managers. The worst that can possibly happen in a given situation is seldom as horrible as the worrier imagined it would be. If the worrier's darkest estimate had been correct, worrying still would have served no purpose except to rob this worrying sales person, or executive, of his persuasive selling power.

Helen Keller, blind and deaf since childhood, could have been justified in dissipating her energy by worrying. Instead she did something to improve her lot. "Self-pity," she said, "is our worst enemy, and if we yield to it we can never do anything wise in the world."

In Washington, D.C., a physician who had many salesmen among his patients had a "health hint" on the wall in his consultation room. It read: "For a long and productive life get a chronic ailment and take good care of it."

Even a minor backache can slow us down. Any ailment that nags at us reduces our persuasive selling power. For this reason the "Three-Way Health Balance" is important to all who sell and to sales management. Those three principles of (a) developing sound health habits, (b) disposing of needless worry, and (c) learning to relax purposefully will strengthen persuasive selling power.

A well-known physical director who conducted classes for businessmen suggested that his pupils "perform" before a mirror at home or in their offices. "Ten minutes before your mirror will provide you with a clear picture of what your body is doing. You will see yourself as your clients see you. Stretch and bend before the mirror. You will notice that exercise becomes more interesting when you perform before the mirror. Tonight, why not add some spice to your before-the-mirror performance by delivering the speech you expect to make in a day or two. Do this before the mirror. Talk to yourself. Are you satisfied with your physical performance? Do your deep breathing exercises before the mirror. All of this sort of performance will be most revealing and beneficial to you."

Principle: Health balance and persuasive selling are closely related. Health balance is the gateway to firing up your sales staff with selling power.

chapter 15

How to Keep Up
Sales "Steam" Through
the Art of Persuasion

Powell Buxton once wrote: "The longer I live the more deeply I am convinced that that which makes the difference between one man and another . . . is energy, invincible determination, a purpose once formed and then death or victory."

In sales management we are, or should be, concerned with harnessing the energy within our sales teams. This is the source of power by which the art of persuasion yields its highest dividends.

The following three-point plan has been effective in keeping up sales "steam." This three-point plan is based on the art of persuasion in sales management:

1. Initiate sales momentum through the art of persuasion in sales management.
2. Increase sales momentum by persuasive selling beginning at the management level.
3. Maintain sales momentum through the art of persuasion.

Sales momentum, once established, must be maintained and constantly increased if we would achieve substantial progress. Progress is a constant thing. This is the primary challenge for sales management.

One imaginative sales manager made this point at an executive conference: "Some of my top men came into this business with doubts about their ability to sell. We encouraged these men. When we detected that they were losing steam we challenged them with new goals. We assured them that management believed in them. This became an additional challenge for them. As a result they got up a new head of steam. They became convinced that they were important to the sales team and to management. By hustling, by making more calls with more purpose and by selling with more conviction they obtained more business. They showed our line to more prospects and with greater impact. They became more and more steamed up as they became more and more aware of their own potentialities."

Another sales manager, with a record for keeping up selling steam, said this: "Some of our new men get business from the start simply because they haven't had time to cultivate the bad habits which lose sales for sales people. I recall one beginner who startled us with his first month's sales record. When asked how he got the business he made a frank and shameless explanation:

" 'I just told my prospects that I was new in the game and that they probably knew more about my products than I did. They seemed to be eager to show me that I was right. They began to tell me about the desirable qualities of our products. Some of them almost shouted to me that my products were the best on the market. In several instances the upshot was that they became sold by themselves. I simply wrote the business. I also left those prospects very much satisfied with themselves. They had a reason to be. Hadn't they really convinced me that they knew more about the line than I did? This sort of satisfaction didn't last forever. On my return calls those prospects expected that I had learned more about my products. This, of course, put it up to me straight. I had to do my own selling for repeat business. But I had one thing in my favor in going after repeat business: My prospects had actually broken the ice for me on my first calls.' "

To keep up sales steam dynamic sales managers persuade their sales people to:

(a) *Be alive* to create sales opportunities.
(b) *Gain,* by merit the confidence of those with whom they deal.
(c) *Study* the possibilities of their line from every angle.
(d) *Develop* an inquiring attitude.
(e) *Be imaginative.*
(f) *Be creative.*

(g) *Be helpful* to each prospect making it easy to make the decision to buy.

(h) *Be persistent* in a constructive way.

The proof of the persuasive power of a sales manager is found in the market place, not in his office. Sales volume, resulting from sales-team action, is the proof that satisfies dynamic sales managers.

Five Effective Ways to Gear Up the Sales Staff

Sales management is a position of *movement.* A steady sales record is not enough. Sales must go up if we are to show progress. To sustain an upward spiral of sales volume dynamic sales managers, either by design or unwittingly, adopt what we choose to call "the A, B, C formula" for persuasive sales management:

(A) Communicate in Two Directions: (1) From management to sales people; (2) from sales people back to management. These two-way lines of communication need to be kept open by persuasive action to promote sales team unity.

(B) Motivate: The fruit of the art of persuasion in sales management is an exciting sales gain. This is movement. This provides motivation for additional gains. Motivation keeps up sales steam.

(C) Action: The ultimate objective of all selling effort is to harvest the fruit of persuasive selling. This is the action which a salesman strives for. This is the result which dynamic sales managers hope for.

Various methods are employed by sales managers to gear up sales people, to make them more productive. In this, sales management must *favorably influence* their sales people. This requires salesmanship of a high order at the management level. A five-point formula which has been tested and has been productive in gearing up sales people follows this pattern.

Keep in Touch with Your Representatives in the Field

The personal in-touch method exerts pressure on men and women to work with more purpose. It gives sales people a feeling of being near to management. They become inspired by the challenge to measure up to the expectations of management.

Use the Memo System

One dynamic sales manager in the insurance field keeps a steady flow of hand-written personal notes going out to his people who are out in the field contacting prospects. These notes may be complimentary. They may also be constructively critical. They may suggest sales possibilities. They may include tips which have come to the attention of the sales manager about prospects in the territory, etc. The memo system is an extension of the keep-in-touch method of gently prodding sales people to "reach for the skies" in selling.

Registered Letters

The U. S. Mail Service attaches considerable importance to registered letters. Your salesman in the field will be alerted if he gets a registered letter from you. "This must be hot," he suggests to himself. You have captured his total attention. The registered letter did the trick. That registered letter may be the means of gearing up a salesman to do an important job more effectively. Your registered letter can make your special instructions more impressive, more persuasive. Thoughtfully and purposefully used registered mail can become a tool for you in gearing up your sales people.

Capitalize on the Unusual

In gearing up your sales staff your objection is to get *action*. Routine is the common enemy of action. When the sales team grumbles, "the same old stuff," then action is stalled. It requires the unusual to seize attention and get action. Isn't that the same doctrine you have been preaching to your sales people? Why then should you, in your executive position, be justified in committing the same sin of falling into the trap of deadly routine which you have been condemning? The alternative: Put life into your sales programs. Capitalize on the unusual to gear up your sales staff.

Get Personal

Don't be misled. You can get too intimate with your sales people, but seldom can you get too personal. Intimacy is a close associate of undue familiarity. As Aesop warned: "Familiarity breeds contempt." The personal touch, however, has great possibilities as a persuasive power. This power is essential in sales management. It is essential in keeping the sales staff geared up to attain its full productive potentiality.

Dynamic sales managers capitalize on the personal touch. They maintain a firm grip on the reins of executive direction. They also avoid entrapment which can result from undue familiarity. By developing a personal interest in the problems, the ambitions, the welfare and the progress of each member of the sales team the sales manager expands and strengthens his executive influence. This is another phase in the art of persuasion in sales management.

How to Get Action by Persuasive Prodding

Action is the end result of purposeful leadership. Persuasive prodding is the action-producing tool of many dynamic sales managers. To prod means to stir up, to urge on. One authority defined legitimate ambition as the urge within us which is "perpetually *prodding* us to do our best."

Sales steam within a group of sales people is maintained by constant prodding. This sort of prodding is done persuasively. In this sense prodding is more subtle than the use of a sharp pointed stick which is the prod that the farmer uses to urge a lazy cow to move forward. Nevertheless persuasive prodding can be nonetheless effective.

The most effective prodding done in sales management is accomplished by developing esprit de corps of a high order within the sales team. Esprit de corps signifies a sense of union, a sense of common purpose, a sense of common interest. This desirable spirit within the sales team multiplies the persuasive selling power of one individual by the total number of persons in the sales team.

The persuasive ingredient which stimulates unified action within the sales team is composed of three things:

1. A definite purpose clearly set forth by persuasive executive leadership.
2. A definite objective specifically defined with persuasive impact for each member of the sales team.
3. A definite plan for attaining the objective which should be exciting, challenging, and persuasive by virtue of promising attainable rewards for the members of the sales team.

The sales manager of a sales promotion specialty house with a nation-wide clientele gets results from his sales people by persuasive prodding in his correspondence with them. For instance, this sales manager in one letter wrote:

"We are in the midst of one of the busiest seasons of the year. This is an ideal time for you to profit. By making more calls and by making these calls more purposeful you can make the figures on your commission checks more attractive. *Drop me a note and let me know about your plans for exploiting our new line* which you now have had time to examine."

Another dynamic sales manager writes to his sales people in this persuasive tone:

"We don't want to appear to be prying into your personal affairs but the new line which we are sampling you today is so loaded with profit possibilities for you that we'd like to know how this opportunity might affect your personal affairs. We'd be delighted to hear from you about the line, about the reaction of your family to it, together with some of your immediate ideas about selling this line to give you a nice increase in your income. More money would be welcomed by you, by your wife and by your two boys, would it not? I'll be looking for a note from you and I'll be watching your sales reports."

Persuasive prodding? Of course it is. And, it is such persuasive prodding which has a way of getting action, such as increasing sales volume.

How Constant Contact Provides Fuel for Persuasive Selling

One word, "contact," and salesmanship are closely tied up in one of the leading dictionaries in this way: "Contact as a verb, meaning to 'get in touch with a person' is a use of the word by salesmen ... The word in this sense is primarily commercial and familiar and should therefore be used infrequently in other circumstances."

This would seem to give us at least one word with a sort of exclusive distinction for our purpose in providing fuel for persuasive selling by *constant contact.*

Effective sales management relies on constant contact to produce sales in volume.

First, communication lines between management and sales teams are established and kept open by *contact.* Likewise, communication lines between sales people and potential customers are established by *contact.* Such contacts are usually personal in nature.

Second, communication lines between sales management and sales teams and between sales people and potential buyers are kept open, operative and productive of sales volume by *constant contact.*

In sales management *constant contact* with the sales force has these five points in its favor:

1. Constant contact is somewhat like a handshake. Even a phone call has a personal touch which can inspire a salesman to exert more effort in his territory.
2. Constant contact is a reminder to members of your sales team that they may be temporarily out of sight but they are not out of mind.

3. Constant contact by sales management nudges the salesman, prods him, persuades him to do a more effective job in selling for his own sake. The contact itself accomplishes this effect. It stimulates self-evaluation and provides motivation for the salesman to become more productive. In this sense, constant contact is a "refueling" operation to increase the selling power of the sales team.

4. Constant contact closes gaps of misunderstanding. It gets sales management and the sales force united in team effort. Purpose is established. Goals are defined. Objectives are clarified. Esprit de corps is encouraged.

5. Constant contact is generalship at its best. An army commander maintains contact with all elements of his command to unify them in winning the battle. A sales manager's aim is similar to that of the general. The sales manager also seeks to unify all elements of his sales force to win his battle for sales volume. This is the objective the dynamic sales manager has established for himself and for his sales team working together as a unified force.

A well-known industrialist once remarked: "Sales people put more spirit into their work if they feel that management is interested in them and in what they are doing. Constant contact with the field force reflects personal interest in their problems and also in their accomplishments. When sales management is constantly in communication with sales people in the field we notice that this results in a steady growth in sales volume on a profitable basis."

The so-called "star" salesman of a selling team in a luxury class automobile agency was asked: "How does your organization show such a steady increase in business against so much active competition?"

This salesman replied: "I believe it is because our sales manager shows that he has a personal interest in each one of us. He works with us, never against us. He doesn't nag. He keeps us under a special type of pressure which makes us want to ring up real sales records. We just know that the head office is watching our record and we don't want to disappoint them. Funny thing, too, is this fact: The spirit our sales manager stirs up in our gang fattens our income at the same time. That's worth something to me and to the rest of the guys."

Examining constant contact from all angles is worth the effort that it requires to make it effective. It does provide fuel for building sales volume. The reason seems to be clear: Constant contact has persuasive power for the sales manager to make him a more dynamic executive, and it has persuasive power for the sales people to make them builders of exciting sales records.

Three New Tips for Maintaining Upward Trends in Sales

While sales managers and their sales people are striving for similar results their viewpoints may vary on how to gain their objectives. For instance: Your sales people eye their individual problems in this way: (a) How to influence specific prospects to buy. (A personal interest involving the art of persuasion.) (b) How to gain access to the most desirable prospects and how to write more volume business. (Again personal interest, and again, the art of persuasion is involved.)

As a sales manager your viewpoint takes a broader slant. (a) You are concerned with motivating a group of sales people to function at top efficiency producing sales in volume and steadily maintaining an upward trend in sales. (This objective summons to your support the art of persuasion in sales management.) (b) You are concerned with influencing each member of your sales team and uniting all of your sales people for total selling power. Of course, you are aware that only by strengthening your motivating influence as a teacher, as a counselor, as a leader will you get production out of your sales team in the desired volume. (Herein lies the key for opening doors to sales in volume. The key is the art of persuasion in sales management.)

Dynamic sales management takes the broad view of sales problems. Dynamic sales managers perceive the combined selling power of a united selling team. The salesman concentrates on getting individual results. The sales manager strives for mass results. Having attained a certain momentum in sales the sales manager becomes aware of another problem: How to maintain an upward trend in sales.

Three tips, gleaned from the records and experiences of sales managers in many fields shed some light on how you may be able to maintain an upward trend in sales in your business.

Build Man-to-Man Sales Power

Assist sales people to drive worry, fear, and all other related ghosts out of their lives. Stimulate your sales team by developing self-confidence in each sales person and by developing their confidence in you as their sales manager. Doing this you show the magnetic power of generalship which wins battles for supremacy in sales management. By neutralizing individual destructive problems which drag sales volume down you provide your sales staff with motivation for team spirit. This is the unified strength which maintains upward trends in sales.

Provide Incentives with Sales Power

Thoughtful sales people quickly detect the bait type of incentive programs. "My people demand something solid to stimulate them to put their maximum sales power into a project," said the sales manager of a paper products firm. "Bait schemes such as credit points and merchandise prizes for doing what they ought to to do without such incentives, and other inducements, have no pulling power in my organization. But, if I present an incentive program which rewards them adequately for notable salesmanship, then I get results. In my language hard cash has more persuasive power with sales people than a piece of ribbon, a lapel button, or some article of merchandise. These things usually are presented for past accomplishments. I prefer to look ahead, not behind me. I try to keep the minds of my sales people on the future and all that it offers them if they can come through with outstanding sales performance."

Encourage Rivalry with Sales Power

Some dynamic sales managers build sales volume on the persuasive power in friendly rivalry within their sales teams. It is human to desire to excel. It is human nature to try to squeeze the full richness out of any situation. Sales management can and does profit by this form of selfishness in sales people. The continuing sales contest, kept alive by constant stimulation, can become a power for maintaining an upward trend in sales.

For sales contest purposes, and to promote friendly rivalry among the sales people, the sales people are divided into three classes by the sales manager of one organization. He makes the classification on the basis of current sales in this way:

Class "A"—The top producers having delivered more than an established figure in sales volume.

Class "B"—Those in this class fall just short of the minimum figure set for Class "A" producers. The Class "B" sales people are designated as the future "threat" to the top producers.

Class "C"—Sales figures of those in this class are below the minimum figure set on the Class "B" group. These are referred to by the sales manager as the potential Class "A" and Class "B" sales people of the future. These he calls the "reserve power."

Note that the power of persuasion is in action in classifying these three groups of sales people. There is a top class but neither a "middle" nor a "low" class. Instead, this sales manager who conducts this successful sales contest calls the Class "B" group a threat (persuasive) to the Class "A" group. Likewise he calls the Class "C" group the "reserve power," implying (persuasively) that anything can be expected from this classification.

The sales manager of a nation-wide firm producing sales stimulators promotes rivalry within his sales force and maintains, thereby, an upward trend in sales volume. His announcement of a new phase in one of his contests contained this persuasive note:

"I assume that one reason you are in our organization is that you are sold on the money-making possibilities of our line. This raises the question: Could you use an extra hundred bucks this month?" He then goes on to detail how bonus money can be earned by his sales people by maintaining an upward trend in sales volume.

The key to maintaining an upward trend in sales is to maintain a high level of persuasive power in sales management.

Tools for Sales Managers Which Nudge Sales Records Higher

Dynamic sales managers design their own tools. With those self-designed tools they nudge sales records higher. Similar tools are available to you for getting greater production out of the efforts of your sales team. Consider these five examples of such tools:

1. The art of persuasion which can be cultivated by you.
2. The "shot in the arm" type of stimulation. A tool for getting sales people to increase production. This tool can be designed and applied by you.
3. Sales producing ideas. These tools can come from your imaginative and creative mind.
4. New and improved techniques for increasing sales. These can be found by you and transmitted to your sales people.
5. Punctuality, dependability and honesty—all tools which can be developed and sharpened for productive use by you.

The art of persuasion heads the list of tools with which sales managers are increasing sales volume. Mastery of this art holds the key to more productive sales-team action.

By mastering the art of persuasion you can: (a) Upgrade your position as an executive; (b) strengthen your leadership; (c) improve your sales training program.

Motivation is the "shot in the arm" tool so effectively used by dynamic sales managers.

Motivation results in sales producing action and combats sluggishness in sales people.

Motivation provides sales people with a purpose. It provides them with worth-while reasons why they should be selling in greater volume. Involved in this are various incentives, which are also tools which serve sales management purposes.

Ideas are the tools which sales managers present to their sales teams for their use. The sales people on their sales teams accept and unite in testing these ideas in the market place. The result: Sales records are nudged higher. Ideas are the tools which create sales and maintain sales volume on an upward trend. The sales manager of a pharmaceutical house said this about ideas:

"We hold regular 'brain storming' sessions. One idea produces another. Soon we have a flood of ideas. The idea catches on that ideas can be provocative and also productive. No sales manager can have a monopoly on ideas. But he can 'pick the brains' of his sales staff. A sales manager can stimulate creative thinking in his sales force. His sales force can become an idea factory which, when generated to think creatively, can gush out ideas that can set up high achievement standards in selling for him."

Techniques are simply the methods by which we go after sales. Sales management, by being alert for new techniques in selling, can nudge sales people to greater production by persuasively introducing them to these new techniques. Newness, in itself, has a persuasive appeal. While we may have read in Ecclesiastes 1:9 that "there is no new thing under the sun," we submit that an old technique, revised, improved and presented with the freshness of timeliness is still a persuasive force in selling.

Through more persuasive presentations of sales techniques as tools which can be used to write business in greater volume sales people are nudged to increase their production.

The tools with which you as sales manager can nudge your sales volume higher include *any means necessary* to motivate, to stimulate, and to train your sales team to sell more of what you have for sale. This requires a high degree of persuasive selling on your part. This is the art of persuasion in sales management in action.

Before adjournment I suggest that you now turn back to Chapter 1 and reread it. This chapter is entitled: "How to Generate Sales Management Power by Persuasion."

I also suggest that you once more complete and evaluate the

self-classification check list included in the first chapter. This check list was designed for capitalizing on our own weaknesses by persuasion.

Dynamic sales managers are developed by critical self-evaluation. They build their own strength by recognizing and capitalizing on their own strong points, their own persuasive qualities, and also on their own weaknesses.

All of this is vital to mastery of the art of persuasion in sales management.

It is also highly constructive, exciting and can become highly profitable.

Index

N

Nervous tension and sales volume, real-
   tionship between, 191-193
New accounts opened, problem of, 156
New territory, exploiting by persuasion,
   81-91
   "bigness," importance of, 83-84
   experience, seeking out for tested
      methods, 85-87
   inexperience, tapping for fresh ideas,
      87-89
   profits, hidden, in acres, people,
      persuasion and sales, 90-91
   sales ideas, testing for persuasive
      power, 89-90
Newcomb, Arthur W., 174
Nightingale, Earl, 167, 179

O

Objectives, clearly defined, as stimulus
   to production, 152-153
Objectives of sales manager, 13
   as source of trouble, 135
On-the-spot surveys to stimulate flow of
   information, 77-78
Optimism, encouraging attitude of in
   salesmen, 94-95
Ostler, Sir William, 112
Over-confidence as cause of losing
   sales, 155

P

Patience, example of overcoming
   weakness in, 21-22
   as essential of "Four P formula," 150
People, hidden profits in, 90-91
   as source of trouble, 134
Perception as essential of "Four P
   formula," 150
Perceptiveness essential for successful
   salesman, 63
Persistence as essential of "Four P
   formula," 150
Person-to-person communication,
   example of overcoming weakness
   in, 19-20

"Personal" and "intimate," difference
   between, 202
Persuasion, hidden profits in, 90-91
Persuasion, women's use of to boost
   sales, 165-166
Peterson, Esther, 159
"Pipe lines" of market information,
   selling team as key to, 71
"Pitches," five persuasive, to stimulate
   salesmen, 33-35
Plain talk, persuasive power in, 117
Plan for sales conference, drafting,
   170-171
Planning, objective, injecting persuasion
   into, 35-39
   conviction, 38
   evaluation and re-evaluation, 38
   goals, 37-38
   knowledge, 38
   time, 36-37
Post mortem method of teaching salesmen how to sell, 116
Pressure, persuasive, how to apply,
   150-151
Pride, personal, appeal to stimulate
   salesman, 34-35
Principles, five, for successful sales
   management, 14
Probationary trial period as method of
   evaluating applicant's selling
   ability, 64
Problem-solving ability, capitalizing on,
   24-25
Problem-solving made easier through
   persuasion, 39-41
Problems for a sales manager, four,
   135-137
   attitude, 136
   manpower, 135-136
   sales resistance, 137
   salesmanship, 136-137
Prodding of sales staff, 203-204
Product-image, favorable, creation of
   by good salesman, 128
Profits, hidden, in people, acres,
   persuasion and sales, 90-91
Public image, creating favorable, 128
Public relations for sales force, improving
   by persuasive selling, 121-131